"Every crime leaves a trace, a piece of the puzzle. We are tirelessly putting those pieces together, and it's only a matter of time before we find the one that leads straight to you."

—Jay C. Rider,
Captain (Retired) Major Crimes Unit, Fort Smith Police Department

"Proverbs 28:1: The wicked flee when none pursueth."

—Chris Boyd,
Major (Retired) Fort Smith Police Department

"This third iteration in the quest for finding justice for Melissa Witt is intense. The perpetrator of this horrific murder needs to be watching over his shoulder. His days are numbered!"

—Robert Bacile
Detective (Retired) Fayetteville Arkansas Police Department

Connected by Fate

LaDonna Humphrey

Genius
Book Publishing

Milwaukee Wisconsin USA

Connected by Fate
Copyright © 2024 LaDonna M. Humphrey

Published by:
Genius Book Publishing
PO Box 250380
Milwaukee Wisconsin 53225
GeniusBookPublishing.com

ISBN: 978-1-958727-30-0

240402 HQ

"A day may come when the courage of men fails, when we forsake our friends and break all bonds of fellowship, but it is not this day."

—J.R.R. Tolkien, The Return of the King

This book is dedicated to Melissa Ann Witt

Foreword by Lexi Kakis

My first email to LaDonna Humphrey was sent on April 29, 2021. At that time, I was just a stranger on the internet—probably one of many inquiring about the Melissa Witt case. I never anticipated that she'd respond, so when I saw that she replied two hours later, I knew she was the real deal. The very next day, I spent hours combing through the case. She answered as many of my questions as best she could without jeopardizing the investigation. From that moment on, I knew LaDonna would soon find justice for Melissa Witt.

My connection to Melissa's case is an untraditional one. I had just started at Uncovered, a crowdsourced cold case database with a true crime community. I had never researched a cold case, yet I volunteered to scour the internet for information on Melissa's case. I had so much to learn. Aside from watching documentaries and listening to podcasts, I didn't know much about cold cases.

Suddenly, Melissa's case would keep me up at night. I never expected her case to leave such a lasting impression. Maybe it was because Melissa vanished the same year I was born. Or maybe it was because we both love Disney and animals. Or perhaps it was because Melissa and I were raised by resilient, empathetic, and loving mothers. Whatever the reason, Melissa is relatable. The more I learned about her, the more I knew she was the type of person I would have been friends with.

I knew I wasn't alone, and that LaDonna felt the same way. In 2022, I had the opportunity to see her advocacy efforts in person. While at Crime Con Las Vegas, she had given me a *The Girl I Never Knew* T-shirt and a #JusticeforMelissaWitt rubber bracelet that I still wear. The bracelet serves as a constant reminder that justice is coming.

LaDonna has poured her entire heart into this case for nearly a decade. She is the quintessential citizen detective. The "Who Killed Missy Witt?" Facebook page created a community of people who care and want to advocate for Melissa. LaDonna harnessed her investigative skills to explore new leads, go down rabbit holes and file Freedom of Information Act (FOIA) requests. Through her writing, she has candidly shared her experiences as a civilian working on a cold case. There are many avenues an investigation can take that the public may never know about. It can be very intense work, both mentally and emotionally, but she never lost sight of that. She worked collaboratively with the Fort Smith Police department to move the case forward. She established trusted relationships with detectives.

This latest book is the direct result of her unwavering commitment to justice for Melissa Witt. Since both of Melissa's parents are deceased, there was no one to continue advocating for her. LaDonna took Melissa's case under her wing and nurtured it. I look forward to the day when Melissa's killer is finally arrested. The smallest piece of information can crack a case. LaDonna has created a blueprint that anyone can follow, as long as they lead with empathy.

Together, we can make a difference.

—Lexi Kakis, Co-Host of Seeking Justice

Table of Contents

Chapter 1: Back to December

A sense of dread tugged at my heart as I pulled into the narrow parking space of the Bowling World parking lot. I turned off the ignition as retired detectives Jay C. Rider and Chris Boyd looked up, acknowledging my arrival with a wave. "Well, here I am," I said out loud as my shoes hit the pavement with a loud thud. I slammed my Suburban door shut and slowly made my way toward them. Even from across the parking lot their somber expressions told a story: The two men were standing in the very spot where Melissa Witt had parked her white Mitsubishi on that fateful December night in 1994.

"Let's get started," Rider directed. He pointed at the stained and worn asphalt as we made eye contact. "This is it. This is where Melissa parked that night."

I scanned the pavement, almost expecting to see the bloodstains left behind from the blitz attack that had left Melissa Witt critically injured. I let out a gasp at the thought, and then immediately turned away from the detectives. I yanked at the oversized sunglasses that were perched on top of my head and quickly put them on in an attempt to hide the tears that were forming. "I'm..." my voice trailed off as I rapidly surveyed the expansive parking lot. "I'm stunned."

Boyd nodded. "It's hard to believe that the son of a bitch attacked her in such close proximity to the building, isn't it?" he barked.

"He was bold," I offered back.

"That he was," Rider added.

As Rider and Boyd dove into a serious discussion about the details surrounding Melissa's abduction and murder, I slipped away quietly. There was something I needed to do. With my head down, I slowly made my way to the entrance of Bowling World. "Sixteen, seventeen, eighteen, nineteen..." I counted. How many steps had separated Melissa Witt from safety on the night she was attacked? "Twenty, twenty-one, twenty-two." I needed to know. At "forty-five" I stopped abruptly in front of the glass doors of Bowling World. "Forty-five steps away from safety." My thoughts shifted into overdrive. Forty-five was also the number of days between the date of Melissa's abduction—December 1, 1994—and the date her body was recovered in the Ozark National Forest—January 13, 1995.

Unsettled by the strange coincidence, I bypassed the retired detectives and hurried back to my Suburban. Inside the safety of my SUV, I slumped down in the driver's seat and reached for a notebook resting on the dashboard. Months earlier, I had carefully written the title "Witt Case" across its cover. I flipped through the pages before landing on what I was looking for—a crude outline of events from December 1, 1994:

6:30-6:40pm—Witness hears a woman shouting "Help me" in the Bowling World parking lot. A young boy, Jeremy, was with his mother at the bowling alley that night. Jeremy reported leaving Bowling World to retrieve a book from his mother's car. He heard a woman scream "Help! Help me!" Underneath the words "Help me" I had written: MELISSA WITT CALLS FOR HELP WHILE SHE IS ATTACKED in bold, red ink.

Directly under those words I had also jotted down this note: Melissa Witt's car keys were located in the parking lot of Bowling World at approximately 7:45pm. The keys were immediately turned in to the front desk inside the building. In the column to the left of these notes I had written: NOBODY noticed the blood spatter on Melissa's keys.

I stared at the words, willing an answer to suddenly appear among my copious notes. "Back to the beginning," I whispered to myself. "If we want answers to this case, we need to go back to the beginning."

A knock on my window interrupted my train of thought. I rolled down the window when I saw Rider standing there. As usual, the exceptionally dressed retired detective was all business. "You coming?" Rider asked. "I want to walk through the timeline of events once again," he said.

I leaned across the console to place the notebook back in its original place on the dashboard.

"I'm coming," I assured him.

"Good. I want to go back to the beginning." My head snapped quickly back in Rider's direction at the sound of his words.

Astounded by the second strange coincidence of the morning, I responded by slowly repeating Rider's own words back to him as I nodded: "Back to the beginning."

❧

As I drove home, Rider's words continued to echo in my head. When I arrived at my office, I decided to once again take a closer look at the events that unfolded on the day Melissa disappeared. From all reports, the day started off routinely. She spent the first part of the morning with her mother, Mary Ann. The honor student would head to Westark Community College next. After that, she went to lunch at the Chick-fil-a in Central Mall with her friend, John, then off to her job as a dental assistant.

Before she left that morning in 1994, Melissa had a minor disagreement with her mother. She had asked to borrow money, and Mary Ann, in an effort to teach her daughter money management, had told her no. Melissa and her mother were especially close. They shared the same beautiful smile, kind heart, and innocent outlook on life. So this argument, while minor, was unusual for them.

Panged with guilt, before Mary Ann left for work that morning, she left a note for Melissa reminding her she would be bowling with her league that evening and offered to buy her a hamburger. She signed the note, "*Love, Mom.*"

At five o'clock that evening, after clocking out of her job as a dental assistant, Melissa discovered that her 1995

Mitsubishi Mirage wouldn't start. After trying to start the car a few times, Melissa gave up and waited with a co-worker until a local businessman, later dubbed the Good Samaritan, gave her car a jump.

Police reports explain how Melissa's dome light was left on by mistake, draining the car battery. Investigators tracked down the Good Samaritan and interviewed him multiple times before ultimately clearing him in the teenager's disappearance and murder.

"People ask about the Good Samaritan all the time because those events leading up to Melissa's abduction seem suspicious," Rider once explained. *"I mean, the Good Samaritan seems suspicious until you realize how many times he was questioned. He was cleared of any suspicion in Melissa's murder."*

We know that, once Melissa's car started, she went home to change out of her uniform. Those clothes were found crumpled on her bedroom floor. Mary Ann Witt was able to determine that her daughter had then donned a white V-neck sweater and jeans.

Melissa must have seen her mom's note, because authorities believe she headed to Bowling World, arriving between 6:30 and 7:00pm. She parked in the northwest corner of the lot, but she never made it inside. There were no cameras to record the events that unfolded in that parking lot that night. Witnesses would later tell police they heard a woman screaming *"Help me!"*

Since Melissa never entered the bowling alley that night, her mother simply thought she had decided to go out with friends instead. Mary Ann went home expecting to see her daughter later that evening. Hours passed and Thursday slowly turned into Friday.

At nine o'clock on Friday morning, Mary Ann reported Melissa as a missing person. When the patrolman took the report that December morning, one of the very first things he asked Melissa's mother was if she and Melissa had argued. Mary Ann told him there had been a small dispute over money. Once he knew about the argument, according to Jay C. Rider, the officer chalked it up to a routine missing person situation. After all, Melissa was considered an adult and it wasn't illegal for her to decide not to come home.

However, Melissa's friends and family knew that it was not like Melissa to take off without telling her mom where she would be. So by Saturday, Melissa's friends and family were frantically passing out flyers, blanketing the River Valley with over 6,000 pleas for help in finding the missing teenager.

Once news stations picked up the story on the search for Melissa Witt, the Fort Smith Police Major Crimes Unit, led by Jay C. Rider, asked to see the missing person report that had been filed. The report had little information. The patrolman knew little more than a 19-year-old girl didn't come home after an argument with her mother. There was no evidence to suggest that Melissa had been abducted. The officer had seen this type of scenario play out hundreds of times before. He was certain Melissa would return home soon. Three days after the initial report of the teenage girl affectionately called "Missy" by her friends and family was marked as a "runaway case," the tide shifted and the Fort Smith Major Crimes Unit had boots on the ground actively searching for the missing teen.

Almost immediately, investigators received a shocking phone call from a bowling alley employee. This call would turn the Witt case upside down. The employee described how at approximately 7:45pm, a set of car keys were found in the parking lot and were turned in to the front desk of Bowling World. The keys held an important clue. The name spelled out on the keychain was "Missy." Even more shocking, no one had noticed the spatters of blood that were slowly drying on the metal keys.

Immediately, investigators began a search to find the person who turned in Melissa's keys on December 1, 1994. After making repeated pleas in partnership with area news stations, after nearly two months, the construction worker who found the car keys came forward. Curtis McCormick had been working at a Tennessee construction site since he had turned in the keys and he had no idea about Melissa's abduction until he returned home to Arkansas.

After his arrival, McCormick's brother was discussing the Witt case with him and that's when the two realized that Curtis was the person police were looking for. When interviewed by investigators, McCormick described how he had spotted the keys when he was distracted by a car with its headlights left on when he arrived at the bowling alley sometime between 7:30 and 8:00 p.m. with his wife and teenage son. According to McCormick, he found the keys laying on the pavement where police later found Witt's car abandoned.

As I reviewed the details of Melissa's disappearance over two decades later, I sat on the floor of my living room, poring over the news footage that captured Melissa's friends and family distributing flyers with her smiling photo and identifying information. I could feel their sorrow. *Where is Melissa?* That question loomed with each news piece. I watched what started out as hopeful interviews with friends and family slowly turned into desperation, despair, and sadness. The answer to their most pressing question "Where is Melissa Witt" had an answer. Her friends and family just didn't know it yet. December would slip quietly into January before the Ozark National Forest would give up the secret that was hidden amongst its dense trees and thorny undergrowth. Melissa Witt was dead. But the smiling faces of her friends and family in this early December news footage had no idea of the horrors that awaited.

I closed my laptop and wondered aloud if Melissa's killer had watched this same footage in the days after her disappearance. I envision him huddled on his mother's expensive couch that cold December weekend, glued to the television, wondering if his terrible secret was safe. When I close my eyes, I can see his smug face, reliving every gruesome detail of Melissa's murder. I imagine him running his murderous fingertips along the steel of her Mickey Mouse watch. I opened my eyes and reached for my iPhone. I opened the Facebook app and scrolled briefly until I found the profile of the man I believe is responsible for killing Melissa Witt. "There you are," I say out loud as I enlarge his profile photo on my phone. I stare at his smiling face and steely eyes. *Did you do it?* I think to myself. *Did you kill Melissa Witt?*

I close the Facebook app as Jay C. Rider's words from our meeting in the bowling alley parking lot flood my mind. "*Back to the Beginning*," he had said. Instinctively, I grabbed one of my notebooks. This one, titled "December 2016," stored a wrinkled copy of an email I had received on December 28, 2016. The one sentence email packed a punch: "*Probably not relevant, but my old college roommate told me he was meeting Melissa the night she disappeared.*" He had no way of knowing it at the time, but this email was beyond relevant. It turns out, his college roommate knew Melissa Witt. Stranger still, his college roommate had actively been contacting me about the Melissa Witt case.

I sank back into the worn and cracked leather of my black office chair and thought back to a description of the Bowling World parking lot given by law enforcement regarding that cold December night. Despite the fact that the dark bowling alley was teeming with cars, there was very little activity happening outside. Inside, however, Bowling World was bustling with bowlers, friends sharing a beer after work, and kids playing video games or pool. The empty parking lot provided the perfect opportunity for a 19-year-old girl to be spirited away under the cloak of darkness.

Like a predator carefully stalking his prey, he watched and waited. His eyes intensely focused on her every move as an unsuspecting Melissa parked her 1995 Mitsubishi Mirage, turned off the engine, and stepped out into the shadows of the Bowling World parking lot. Suddenly, Melissa is caught off guard. She looks up in a mix of fear and surprise. But it's too late. His sharp eyes are locked on the target. He is ready to strike. And then, it happens. The hunter makes his move.

Chapter 2: The Great War

The attack on Melissa that Thursday night at Bowling World is often described by investigators as a "blitz attack." This sudden, intense, and violent act is aimed at one purpose: overwhelming a victim quickly. The very nature of a blitz attack is both abrupt and forceful, leaving the victim very little chance to react or defend themselves. This is important to consider when looking at how offenders that carry out murders. Killers are categorized in one of three ways.

The first category is known as the organized offender. This type of killer generally hides or disposes of a body, often preselecting a dumpsite prior to committing their crimes. And this type of criminal avoids leaving any evidence behind. An organized killer will typically have three crime scenes: 1) Where he met the victim, 2) Where the victim was killed, and 3) Where the victim was buried/hidden.

The second category is known as a disorganized offender. This type of criminal acts impulsively and rarely utilizes a well-rehearsed plan to gain their victim's confidence. Instead, they act suddenly and violently in order to overwhelm their victim. Their crime is almost always messy and chaotic. A disorganized killer tends to leave the body at the crime scene, often engaging in sexual contact with the victim post-mortem.

The last type of criminal, known as a "mixed" offender, leaves behind a variety of haphazard messages at two or more locations. At the initial crime scene, his actions are often frenzied and messy, indicating he only has a very small measure of control over his deep-seated, violent fantasies. The second location is usually the place where he hides or buries the body. This crime scene is almost always more meticulous and controlled, and he leaves behind little to no evidence.

Melissa's assault in the parking lot was the truest definition of a frenzied, messy, haphazard attack by a "mixed offender" who had very little control of the crime scene. Her killer was impulsive and sloppy. He left too much evidence behind. Pools of blood, a crushed hair clip, an earring, and Melissa's car keys were all left in the parking lot. The killer's hurried attack was clearly his way of quickly overpowering a defenseless 19-year-old girl in a fit of rage.

The second location in the Ozark National Forest, however, was much more controlled. He chose a location an hour away from the bowling alley that allowed him to blend seamlessly into the darkness. It was here, on a mosaic of decaying leaves, pine needles, and frozen underbrush, that he strangled Melissa Witt. And it was here, under the dense canopies and foreboding shadows of the national forest that he shifted from a frenzied, disorganized killer to a calculated mastermind, meticulously stripping away Melissa's clothing, shoes, and beloved Mickey Mouse watch.

Investigators also believe that Melissa knew her killer very well. In fact, Jay C. Rider and Chris Boyd are convinced that his intentions that night were centered around confronting Melissa, or trying to charm his way back into her good graces.

လ

"I believe that he knew where Melissa would be and when she would be there," explained Boyd one afternoon in late 2017. "In fact, I think he was already there at the bowling alley waiting for Melissa to visit her mother like she so often did."

"I think you are absolutely right," I replied. "After all, it was common knowledge among Melissa's friends that her mom bowled every Thursday night as part of a women's league. And everyone close to Melissa knew that she often spent her Thursday evenings watching her mom bowl."

Boyd nodded his head in agreement. "That's why I don't believe for one second this guy drove to a crowded bowling alley with the intention of kidnapping and killing her," he explained.

"Instead, he drove there to confront her," Boyd emphasized by raising his eyebrows. "And that plan, well, it went terribly wrong."

The initial meeting in the parking lot between Melissa and the man who would eventually take her life escalated quickly from a simple confrontation to a full-blown argument. Witnesses reported hearing raised voices and a woman shouting. Investigators also believe that Melissa's resistance to the man's advances resulted in him either violently shoving her to the ground or striking her in the head. One afternoon, as Jay C. Rider and I reviewed the Witt case, he echoed Boyd's sentiments on what happened that December night in 1994. "I think he wanted her to go with him," Rider explained. "But I don't believe he ever intended for the events that night to lead to her death."

An 11-year-old boy, who was with his mother at Bowling World that night, would eventually come forward to report that, when he went out to retrieve a book from their car between 6:30 and 7:00 p.m. he saw a couple together in the parking lot and then he suddenly heard the woman scream, "Help me!" If his timeline is accurate, it points to an attack that took place almost immediately upon Melissa's arrival at Bowling World.

I've played this scenario out in my mind dozens of times: He approaches Melissa in the dimly lit parking lot with a posture of dominance and control. Feeling cornered and vulnerable, and exasperated by the unwanted advances, Melissa rejects him, wounding his fragile ego. The two argue and, when she will not acquiesce to his egotistical demands, he lashes out by either violently shoving Melissa and causing her to hit her head, or by actually striking her in the head with a blunt object.

Weeks later, after Melissa's body was discovered in the Ozark National Forest, the medical examiner's report described the injury she suffered at the bowling alley as "non-fatal trauma to the side of her head." As seen by the amount of blood that was eventually found in the Bowling World parking lot, the blow to Melissa's head bled profusely. Alarmed and enveloped in a haze of frenzied terror by the sight of blood, Melissa's attacker did not stop to consider that even minor cuts on the head often bleed heavily due to the amount of blood vessels close to the surface of the skin. Instead of showing remorse or compassion, he is consumed by rage and fear.

He makes the decision to snatch Melissa up and load her injured body into the back of his vehicle. And then, according to Chris Boyd, "the killer began driving and trying to figure out in his unorganized mind what he should do next."

Later, an FBI profiler would analyze the Witt case and determine that the mixed offender who kidnapped and killed Melissa Witt was also most likely a "beer drinking, womanizing, country boy who loved the outdoors." And while Chris Boyd and Jay C. Rider agree with the FBI assessment, they also believe that the killer knew *both* Melissa Witt and the Ozark National Forest very, very well.

ço

Flashbacks of Boyd's words along with the details of what happened that night at the bowling alley often sneak into my consciousness and play on repeat when I least expect it. As I sat in the Fort Smith Police Department conference room one sunny spring morning, Boyd's words crept into my mind. He had said, "This seems to be the most likely reason Melissa's body was placed where it was. Her killer was very familiar with the Ozark National Forest. This was not some random serial killer. He knew Melissa. And he knew our area," Boyd continued. "And I would put my money on the fact that he's still living nearby."

I skimmed through Melissa's diary. "Maybe he isn't the right guy for me," Melissa wrote.

I flipped to another entry. "He tried to make up excuses why he didn't call."

My heart raced. Could these diary entries be significant?

"He called and griped at me," she wrote. "I'm not calling him again. He can kiss my butt."

A wave of nausea overtook my body as I stared at the last diary entry. The young man Melissa described in her diary checked all the boxes:

1. He was someone Melissa knew well.
2. He showed signs of being a controlling, narcissistic womanizer.
3. It was clear, based on her own words penned in her diary, that Melissa was no longer interested in entertaining his foolish games and she was ending all communication.

He must have sensed her determination to end the relationship, because just days before her abduction and murder, she writes of how he was trying to get back in her good graces.

"This…. This scenario could be the very reason why he showed up at the bowling alley that night!" I shouted across the conference room to Brad Marion, the current detective on Melissa's case.

"What is it?" Marion asked.

I marched across the room and carefully placed Melissa's diary in his outstretched hand. I silently pointed to the entry, my eyes pleading for him to read it.

Marion looked up from Melissa's delicate script with a serious look in his eyes. I pressed harder. "Over half the killings of American women are related to intimate partner violence," I explained urgently, reaching for my backpack.

"I am not telling you anything you don't already know," I said, yanking a report from a folder buried inside my bag. "But look at this article. The CDC analyzed the murders of over 10,000 women in 18 states and of those murders, 93 percent of those women were killed by a former romantic partner."

Marion nodded his head.

"Get this," I said, touching Marion's arm to emphasize my point. "In just over a third of those deaths, the couple had argued right before the murder took place," I explained hurriedly.

"She knew her killer," I said confidently.

Just as Marion opened his mouth to reply, the door to the conference room flew open.

In unison, Marion and I turned our heads just as Jay C. Rider made his entrance. After years of friendship, Rider immediately noticed the look of determination chiseled on my face. "What is it, Humphrey?"

I raised my eyebrow as I blurted out the answer to Rider's question. "She knew her killer," I repeated.

"Of course she did," Rider replied without hesitation.

"And his name…" Rider paused as he pointed in our direction. "His name is in that diary."

Chapter 3: Ozark National Forest

On January 13, 1995, two animal trappers, about 15 miles north of Ozark, stumbled upon what they believed could be a mannequin lying face down in the woods about 30 feet off the main road. According to interviews, the two men had driven this road the day before and there had been nothing there. Upon closer inspection, the men were horrified to discover that the strange figure lying in the Ozark National Forest was actually the decomposing nude body of a young, white female. Dental records would later confirm that, after 45 long days, Melissa Ann Witt had finally been found.

Over twenty years later, as I accompanied law enforcement along State Highway 23, also known as the "Pig Trail," on our way to the remote Forest Service Road 1551 where Melissa Witt's body was discovered, I was overcome with sadness. It was impossible to enjoy the beauty of the natural scenery that surrounded us during our trek through the Ozark National Forest. My every thought was on Melissa Witt and how her final journey on this stretch of highway led to the unthinkable: her murder.

As we turned off Highway 23 and onto Shores Lake Road, I stared intently into the trees that lined the lonely dirt road that would lead us deeper and deeper into the Ozark National Forest. The trees, I thought to myself, held a precious gift—a form of memory that transcended common understanding. Trees hold memories in their rings and each ring is a testament to a year in their life. Each ring, like a chapter of a book, holds important stories as a reminder of their individual experiences, recording such things as periods of drought, abundance, fire, struggles, growth, and even disease.

But beyond physical memory, trees also hold a biological memory. This is demonstrated in the way they become more resilient in response to things such as stress or extreme climates. The way trees learn to adapt is also a form of memory that records their interaction with the world around them. These tall, silent witnesses not only observe activity around them, but they also absorb the energy that is near them. As we moved along the winding road, I watched as sunlight peeked through the canopy of leaves overhead and I quietly wondered, *What secrets did these hushed giants hold in their memory from December 1994?*

As we approached our destination, the dense trees quickly shifted into a wide expanse, revealing the Baptist Vista Church Camp. The camp, established in 1949 by the churches of the Clear Creek Baptist Association, has one stated purpose: a place to offer a camping experience for people while also giving them the opportunity to hear the gospel of Jesus Christ

The 65-acre camp is split into two main areas: the recreation field and the main campus. The recreation fields provide 35 acres for campers to swim, hike, and play organized sports. This area is bordered by both the Ozark National Forest and the beautiful and mysterious Mulberry River.

The main campus is just a few miles from the location where Melissa's body was found, and it includes a pool, a craft building, a preschool building with a fenced-in yard, a play yard, a nurse's station, two worship tabernacles, and over 20 cabins ranging in capacity from 8 to 62 people with a max capacity of 600 campers at one time. The camp, open to visitors during the summer, is closed for activities in the late fall and winter months. In December of 1994, the camp, as usual, was closed.

As the camp slowly faded into the rearview mirror, a cloud of heavy silence settled over us. The logging road was just ahead. Our driver turned on his blinker as he prepared to make his way onto Service Road 1551. The incessant "click, click, click, click" of the blinker was jolting. It disrupted both the quiet seclusion of the lonely forest and our morose thoughts about a girl we never knew.

"Shut it off," I demanded almost instinctively. I paused and then added, "please."

The driver, stunned by the weight of emotion my voice carried, simply nodded his head and stopped the clicking blinker just as he turned on to the narrow, unpaved path. Engulfed in silence once again, my attention was directed to the rough and rocky terrain of the logging road. The road, shrouded by towering trees and dense woods, jostled and bounced our car as the tires crunched over the uneven terrain. The car's engine hummed steadily as we carefully navigated large rocks and fallen branches before abruptly stopping. I gazed out the window, and immediately recognized our location. I'd seen this place before in crime scene photos. We were parked just steps away from where Melissa's body was discovered on January 13, 1995.

My stomach lurched as we exited the car and stepped onto the rugged landscape that was littered with fallen leaves and pine needles. I took a deep breath. The scent of moist earth hung heavy in the air. The area, untouched by the passage of regular vehicles and modern civilization, was eerie. It was hard to believe that this place, known only by wildlife as home, once cradled the body of a young 19-year-old woman between its fallen leaves and thorny undergrowth.

As I stood there on a patchwork of earthy browns and fading greens, listening to the detectives describe Melissa's murder, I recalled her obituary. "The funeral for Melissa 'Missy' Ann Witt, 19, of Fort Smith Arkansas will be 2 p.m. January 17 in Grand Avenue Baptist Church. A 1993 graduate of Northside High School, she was a dental assistant and member of Grand Avenue Baptist Church. She also attended Westark Community College where she was a member of the Pride." I glanced around the serene forest, brimming with oak, hickory, and patches of pine and cedar trees, and realized this was the ultimate paradox:

A breathtaking landscape was home to the most heinous of crimes—the murder of a 19-year-old girl.

We know that Melissa died in the Ozark National Forest because the medical examiner reported her official cause of death as "asphyxiation by strangulation." Leaves and soil found in Melissa's airway indicated she had been strangled face down and she had inhaled debris from the forest floor as she fought for her life. Laboratory testing on the debris found in Melissa's airway told investigators an important story: It was native to the Ozark National Forest. This told investigators that she had been killed at or near the location where her body was discovered.

I would also learn through my investigation into the Witt case that dozens of similar crimes occurred in national parks in the mid-1990s. One of the first cases that comes to mind is that of Julianne (Julie) Williams and Laura (Lollie) Winans. On Sunday May 19, 1996, the two women excitedly embarked on a backpacking trip in the Virginia Shenandoah National Park with their furry companion, a golden retriever named Taj.

Julie, 24, and Lollie, 26, connected by their love of the outdoors, pitched their tent off a Shenandoah National Park horse trail. The innocent spot they chose, next to a mountain stream, turned out to be a deadly mistake. Investigators believe the continuous trickling din of the water most likely drowned out the sound of the approaching footsteps that marched to the slow, steady rhythm of murder.

With no contact from either Julie or Lollie, Thomas Williams, Julie's father, reported his daughter missing on

May 31, 1996. Park Rangers began an extensive search, and after locating Julie and Lollie's car, they combed trail corridors in the general area where they believed the women could be. Despite their best efforts, only Taj, the golden retriever was discovered wandering the national park alone. There was no sign of Julie or Lollie.

The next evening, on June 1, 1996, a horrific discovery was made. Julie and Lollie's nude bodies were found at their campsite. The women had been bound, gagged, and their throats slit. There were no signs of sexual assault. Through my research I would learn that their campsite was a mere ten-minute walk from the Skyland Lodge, a popular gathering place with a bar and restaurants. And yet, nobody heard a thing. After committing the brutal murders, the killer slipped quietly away into the tranquil, picturesque national park.

Another case of note is the 1996 disappearance of Sheila Kearns. This time, the setting was the beautiful Mount Rainier National Park in Washington. At the time, Sheila was 43 years old, and she was working as an employee of the national park in an attempt to "reset" her life. Co-workers said that Sheila absolutely loved her job so when she didn't show up for work one fall morning, they knew something was terribly wrong. Sheila was last seen at the National Park Inn at Longmire around 6:00 p.m. on October 4, 1996.

Once she was reported missing, Park rangers combed the park extensively for three days but found nothing of significance. Sheila had simply disappeared without a trace. However, that changed in May of 1997 when Sheila's remains were found scattered in a 300-yard area near Longmire Camp. To this day, investigators remain baffled that Sheila's remains were found in an area that had been thoroughly searched when she first went missing.

Unexplained circumstances in cold cases are not unusual. Even Melissa Witt's unsolved murder has its fair share of odd occurrences: A strange phone call came in to the Fort Smith Major Crimes Unit a day or two prior to the discovery of Melissa's body in the Ozark National Forest. The female caller, described as having a thick Southern accent, left a message one evening. In the message, she could be heard saying, "*Go ahead and tell them what you found.*" There also was a younger male voice, also with a thick Southern accent, who was reported saying, "*No, I can't,*" and then the phone disconnected.

Some believe that the young man who was part of the mysterious phone call could also be related to another very bizarre circumstance in the Witt case. After Melissa's body was discovered in the Ozark National Forest, crime scene investigators thoroughly searched the surrounding area. They were shocked to discover indentations behind a large headstone-like rock positioned between two small trees that revealed Melissa's body had initially been hidden there. According to police records and interviews, her decomposing body had visible marks where someone had grabbed hold of her and dragged her in order to move her closer to the road. As I recalled the gruesome crime scene photos that are burned into my psyche, I shivered. Moving a body that is in advanced stages of decomposition is not for the faint of heart. What type of person is capable of that kind of atrocity?

☙

As I sat with retired investigators Boyd and Rider over lunch several weeks later, we discussed the possibility of the strange phone call being connected to Melisa's lifeless body being moved. "Did a hunter discover Melissa's body in the woods and move it from behind the rock so she could be found? Was he scared he would be blamed for the murder?" I asked.

I made eye contact with both men and immediately hurled two more questions in their direction, "Did her killer, in a moment of remorse, come back to move Melissa's body so she could be found and given a proper burial? Who was the person responsible for the puzzling phone call made to the Fort Smith Major Crimes Unit?"

Boyd locked eyes with Rider, gesturing for him to respond. "It's unfortunate, but unless someone comes forward, we may never know who made that phone call," Rider explained. "We have done everything in our power to find them. We have made pleas through the media and we have followed up on every lead that could point to their identity. This part of the case may remain a mystery."

I frowned at Rider's response and threw down my napkin. "This is so frustrating!" I exclaimed.

"Tell us about it." Boyd sighed.

During lunch, Boyd took another bite of his sandwich while Rider jumped into the conversation. "Melissa's killer was either a local or someone who frequented the area from out of state to hunt, hike, camp, or fish. He could have disposed of her body anywhere, but he chose this remote location. And he chose it for a reason. He either came back to revisit the crime scene and he moved Melissa so she could be found, or someone else, also familiar with the area, stumbled upon her body and decided to move her."

I turned away from the table to gaze out the window. As I watched the steady flow of traffic on the busy city street outside, I tried to process the ghastly nature of this horrible crime. Only a monster, I reasoned, could use his bare hands to choke the life out of an innocent teenage girl, then return weeks later to put his hands on her once more in order to relocate her corpse. These thoughts sent a deep pang of grief for Melissa's mother like a shockwave through my body. *Poor Mary Ann*, I thought to myself. It was heartbreaking to think that before her death, Mary Ann had spent sixteen years, three months, and nineteen days tormented by the circumstances surrounding the murder of her beloved daughter. *Melissa deserves justice*, I thought. *But so does Mary Ann.*

❧

A week later inside a small cafe in Ozark, Arkansas, my thoughts remained on Mary Ann Witt and the discovery of her only child's body in the national forest. Determined to get answers, I made the trip to Franklin County that morning with one purpose: justice for Melissa Witt. Just before I made the hour-long trek to the small, picturesque city located in the Arkansas River Valley, I placed a call to action on social media: "Our team will be in Ozark, Arkansas today in our quest for Justice for Melissa Witt. If you have information about the 1994 abduction and murder of Melissa, and you would like to meet with our investigative team in person, please send us a private message to set up an interview." As my team sat inside the rustic cafe of this small Arkansas town, surrounded by its rich history and natural beauty, our focus was set on collecting any secrets this charming little town could offer up about Melissa's murder.

To our surprise, not long after our arrival at the cafe, a steady stream of people arrived—everyone from concerned elderly residents to young adults seeking answers. Each person had a different background and reason for meeting with our team. The atmosphere was a mix of curiosity, anxiety, and anticipation. I watched as people nervously fidgeted with their hands and chatted with their neighbors about what might have happened to Melissa in the woods in December of 1994.

I sat nestled in a corner table, listening attentively to each person who stopped by. People shared concerns about local crime, tales about suspicious characters, and frightening long-standing community rumors and legends. Each person brought a unique story that reflected that diverse tapestry of life in a small town; however, no one offered up what we were looking for: information about the Witt case.

Discouraged, I shuffled my papers into my backpack and prepared to leave. As I stood from my seat, a woman with ill-fitting, wrinkled clothing walked through the doors. With her shoulders hunched and her gaze lowered, she avoided eye contact as she asked the woman at the counter, "Is LaDonna Humphrey still here?"

"Yeah," the waitress pointed, "she's over there."

As the woman approached, I immediately noticed her untidy, tangled hair. Her faded, smudged makeup added to the overall disarray of her appearance. She walked toward me with an expression that carried a mix of fatigue and distress. With her brow furrowed, she stopped just feet away from our table and said, "LaDonna Humphrey?"

I glanced around the room before extending my hand to the unkempt stranger. "Nice to meet you. I'm LaDonna," I offered with a smile. "Please," I motioned, "sit down."

The woman took a seat at the table, her hands tightly wrapped around her purse, her posture closed off and tense. "I don't want you to use my name," she said through tightly pressed lips.

"Of course not," I agreed. "We will keep your name confidential."

"I have to live in this God-forsaken town," she whispered quietly. "I don't want no trouble."

"We don't either," I said soothingly.

Seemingly indifferent to my assurances, she reached into her bag and extracted a worn obituary. "Have you heard about him? About Steve?" she asked.

"I don't think so," I responded. Our eyes locked. "May I?" I asked as I reached across the table.

The woman pushed the tattered booklet in my direction. "I don't want no trouble," she repeated.

I carefully scanned the first few lines of the document: "... of Ozark, Arkansas, died Tuesday August 4, 2015 in Ozark. He was a mechanic…"

Before I could finish, the woman abruptly stood up. "You should look into him. He tried to kidnap a girl in Crawford County in December of 1994," she said. She paused before adding, "I think there were others." And without another word, the woman silently exited the cafe.

Without missing a beat, I extended my arm across the surface of the table toward my cell phone. In one smooth motion, I picked up the phone and dialed Jay C. Rider. The phone rang twice before I heard the booming sound of his voice. "What'cha got?" Rider asked.

"Stephen Pledger," I responded. "Who is he?"

Chapter 4: The Secrets We Keep

For the next half hour, Rider described in detail his account of Pledger's arrest and subsequent charges for the attempted abduction of a young woman in Van Buren, Arkansas in December 1994. "At the time of his arrest, Pledger was a 33-year-old mechanic living in Ozark." Rider explained thoughtfully.

"Let me guess," I responded. "He was also an avid outdoorsman."

"Believe it or not, he was," Rider said flatly. "And he was very familiar with the Ozark National Forest. But not only that, after attempting to abduct this woman from the parking lot, he used a rope to try and tie her up."

"Wow!" I exclaimed. "That certainly seems to indicate he came prepared to abduct her."

Rider agreed. "It's definitely strange. And that is exactly why Dale Best with the Arkansas State Police alerted us to the attempted kidnapping. Best believed it was possible that the two incidents could possibly be connected."

I can certainly see why, I thought to myself. *After all, what are the chances that two young women, in towns that are less than 20 miles from each other, would be plucked out of dark parking lots just weeks apart?* A cold shiver went down my spine.

After my conversation with Rider, I dove into every shred of information available on Stephen Pledger. Court records defined his 1994 crime as an act of "false imprisonment." My heart raced. *Is it possible that Pledger was trolling for another young girl because the abduction of Melissa Witt had taken an unexpected and deadly turn?*

With little information available to the public on Pledger, I turned to social media and posted the following: "Did you know? In December of 1994, in the weeks after the abduction of Melissa Witt, a man from Ozark tried to kidnap a young woman from a parking lot in Van Buren. Thankfully, his attempt failed. It turns out, the man was an avid hunter who is very familiar with the Ozark National Forest. Prior to his death in 2015, he denied any involvement in the murder of Melissa Witt."

The response to my Facebook post was both quick and passionate. As messages poured in, I was stunned by the cloud of suspicion that still hung heavy over Pledger after all these years. Even more, I was astonished by the fact I never used Pledger's name in my Facebook post, and yet, the memory of his crime still elicited a strong, zealous response from the community. Unfortunately, however, very little concrete evidence was provided. Instead, the information received was based largely on unsubstantiated rumors.

Through the years, investigators did remain curious about Pledger's possible connection to Witt's abduction and murder, so much so that in the weeks leading up to his death, a detective sat with Pledger and his family in case he made a "dying declaration." Pledger, however, did not confess to Melissa's abduction and murder before his death.

It's also important to keep in mind that regardless of law enforcement's efforts to try to find a connection between Stephen Pledger and the Witt case, none was ever found. Outside of the attempted kidnapping in Van Buren, there is no evidence that points to Pledger's involvement in Melissa's murder. And a cloud of suspicion, no matter what the circumstances may be, certainly does not equate to guilt. So if Pledger, by chance, was involved in Melissa's murder, he carried that secret with him to his grave.

The attempted kidnapping in Van Buren isn't the only sinister secret that the River Valley area holds. Harold Solomon, a self-proclaimed "outlaw" and convicted rapist, left a trail of horrific crimes all across Arkansas, Oklahoma, and Missouri.

On the afternoon of Sunday, November 24, 1996, Heather Wilson drove to the Branson, Missouri Wal-Mart to purchase a few groceries and household items. After leaving the store, Wilson returned to her car. As she tried to unlock it, Harold Solomon seized the opportunity. He grabbed the car door and forced Wilson into her vehicle. Once inside the car, Solomon brandished a sheathed knife, while simultaneously promising the frightened young woman that if she complied with his demands, she would not get hurt.

Next, Solomon shoved Wilson into the passenger's seat and sped out of the parking lot toward Table Rock Lake. As he turned down a dead-end road, Solomon demanded that Wilson remove all of her clothing. He then parked the car, walked to the passenger's side, dropped his pants, and demanded that she perform oral sex on him. When the sexual assault was over, Solomon directed Wilson to get dressed then forced her into the trunk of her car.

Solomon, however, was far from finished with his evil plan. According to reports, he then drove Wilson's car for approximately another seven to ten minutes before stopping on a gravel road and removing her from the trunk. He then instructed Wilson to squint her eyes as he blindfolded her and led her into a mobile home. There, he changed Wilson's blindfold and forced her to undress again. Solomon then proceeded to brutally and repeatedly rape the frightened young woman.

After the violent sexual assault was over, Solomon led Wilson back to her car, removed her blindfold, and ordered her back into the trunk. He then drove back to the Walmart parking lot where he assured Wilson that she could call for help after counting to one hundred.

After counting to one hundred, Wilson used her cell phone to call her boyfriend, and then began pounding on the trunk, pleading for help. A passerby heard the terrified screams and ran inside the store. With the help of a Walmart manager, Wilson was freed from the trunk of the car just as the police arrived.

Two weeks later, a highway patrolman in Taney County, Missouri attempted to stop a vehicle driven by Solomon. Despite his efforts to evade state police, Solomon was captured and placed under arrest. On December 13, 1996, Wilson was shown five color photos of Taney County inmates and asked if she could identify her attacker. Wilson was quick to tell police that she was certain four of the five men were not the man who had kidnapped and brutally assaulted her. However, she was not sure about the photo of the fifth man. According to Wilson, she was unable to make a positive determination if Solomon was her attacker from the photo she was provided. "I need to see his eyes," Wilson explained.

Law enforcement acted quickly, putting together a lineup of four of the five men that were in the original photos given to Wilson. Almost immediately, Wilson identified Harold Solomon as the man responsible for her kidnapping and rape. "I can see his eyes now," Wilson reported to police. "And I am certain that is the man who attacked me."

This was not, however, the only crime Solomon was responsible for. The same year of Wilson's attack, a governor's warrant sought to extradite Solomon for failure to appear on a charge of possession of meth with the intent to deliver in Sebastian County, Arkansas. Later, he was also charged in Boone County, Arkansas with aggravated robbery, theft of property, and six counts of rape. Then, in July of 1996, Solomon was charged once again, this time in LeFlore County, Oklahoma, for possession of methamphetamines. Solomon's crime spree, however, was far from over. In 1997, he was charged with the attempted kidnapping of a woman in Crawford County. During the commission of this crime, just as he had done with Heather Wilson, Solomon flashed a knife at his victim while trying to force her into a vehicle.

Solomon's criminal history, however, existed long before the 1990s. From 1982-1988, he served time in prison after pleading guilty to rape, assault with attempt to rape, and burglary. Then, in 1989 Solomon received an 80-year prison sentence in LeFlore County for rape and kidnapping. In 1994, the court of appeals overturned his conviction and released Harold Solomon back into society.

Solmon's arrests and convictions for drugs, kidnapping, and rape, combined with his 1994 early release from prison, piqued my interest. I wanted to learn all I could about Solomon's history. My search immediately led me to a 1998 news piece published by the Springfield Missouri News Leader. The article was a treasure trove of information about the career criminal. In it, I was astonished to read the following: "Authorities say Solomon also has victims in Arkansas and Oklahoma."

Shocked, I kept reading.

"I think he's a serial rapist and he will rape repeatedly again if he's ever turned loose," said Don Swan, a Taney County sheriff's investigator. "I also think he's an extreme danger to society and to any woman who may resist his advances."

"Resist his advances," I repeated aloud to myself. Wasn't this the *exact* scenario investigators suspected in the

Melissa Witt case——that she had spurned the advances of the man that attacked her?

☙

The next day, as I drove through the lush greenery and rolling hills of the Ozark mountains on my way to the River Valley from Northwest Arkansas, my thoughts were focused on Harold Solomon.

As I made my way into Fort Smith, a city once regarded as the gateway to the Wild West, I was excited for the task ahead—another deep dive into Melissa's case file. This time, Jay C. Rider and I would be working together to comb through the mounds of paperwork in the unsolved murder investigation. Our goal was to search for any shred of information that could help put this cold case to rest once and for all.

When I arrived at the Fort Smith Police Station, Rider was already upstairs, sipping coffee and making small talk with a group of detectives. As I approached, I smiled and waved at Rider. "Damn!" I said jokingly as I rolled my eyes. "I'm shocked you made it on time, let alone early."

"Oh, fuck you, Humphrey!" Rider laughed. "Let's get to work." He pointed toward the conference room as he continued to chuckle.

"Ready when you are, sir," I said as I followed him down the hallway.

Once inside, our jovial nature was replaced with somber determination. Without so much as a word,

Rider and I each grabbed a stack of papers and got right to work. Almost immediately, a report written by Sgt. L. Lonetree entitled "Supplementary Investigation Report. Melissa Witt's Found Vehicle" caught my eye. As I scanned through the pages, I stumbled upon something in the report I hadn't noticed before: "Just looking at the vehicle nothing appeared to be out of the ordinary. The only thing that appeared slightly suspicious was the fact the rear Arkansas license plate was bent on the lower right-hand corner of the plate. This will be collected and later processed for latent fingerprints."

"Interesting," I said out loud. "Did the killer come back to the bowling alley to remove Melissa's license plate?" I asked Rider as I handed him the report. "Maybe he hoped he could delay the car being identified by removing her plates?"

Rider handed the report back to me and said, "Without a screwdriver?"

I shrugged my shoulders. "If our theory is right, and this guy was disorganized and out of control at the first crime scene, perhaps once he was in control, like he was in the Ozark National Forest, he came back to remove the license plate," I reasoned.

"Maybe," Rider replied. "For now, let's just make a note to revisit this topic again. It definitely warrants more discussion."

I nodded in reply and continued to comb through the neatly typed pages of Lonetree's report: "This vehicle appeared to have been driven into its last resting place on the Bowling World parking lot from a western direction. The vehicle was facing south, and the front tires were turned just slightly to the right, as if the vehicle had been pulled into the space from a western direction. The vehicle was about 110'9" east of the western edge of the bowling world parking lot. The vehicle was in the tenth space out of the twenty-three spaces, as you count from the western edge of the parking spaces. There are a total of fourteen rows of parking spaces, and seven columns. In each of the columns there are two rows, each row faces the other. One row is facing north, and the other row faces south."

I jotted down Lonetree's detailed description and moved onto the next page: "Det. John Wagner got a key, and we checked the inside of the trunk. The inside was very clean and contained one box—a cardboard box, with a foot pump in it, one set of jumper cables, and an answering machine. The answering machine was collected and will be checked to see if there are any messages on it at a later date and time. We next checked the interior of the vehicle. On the rear bench seat was a maroon backpack with black handles and green trim—a Jansport Backpack. Inside the backpack were two sociology books, one blue mead notebook, and one red three ring binder notebook. Inside the first small, zipper compartment we found a handwritten note. The note included directions on how to get to an apartment in Dallas, Texas. Det. Wagner took the note and made contact with the authorities in Texas to have the apartment checked for Melissa Witt. As the note was investigated, the owner of the apartment in Dallas is in Fort Smith helping the family look for Melissa."

When the note was discovered in Melissa's backpack, it initially appeared to be a possible lead in the case. However, upon further investigation, law enforcement learned that the owner of the apartment and the subject of the note was a young man named Travis, a close friend of Melissa's. When authorities reached out to interview Travis, they learned he was already in Arkansas assisting with the search for his dear friend.

Like others in this investigation, Travis was extensively interviewed to determine if he had any information about Melissa's disappearance. After cooperating fully with investigators, Travis was cleared of any suspicion in the case.

Rider and I made small talk as I flipped through the report. "The concentration of evidence was located between columns A and B, Rows 1, 2 and 3." I read aloud.

Rider paused and looked up from the notebook he was reviewing. "You might consider taking notes on that," he suggested. "That information could prove valuable for the documentary."

I took his advice and jotted down some notes as I rifled through the remaining few pages in the stack. The last report, titled "Crime Lab," was a carefully detailed spreadsheet of items investigators collected in the Ozark National Forest. The neatly typed columns were labeled Evidence, Description of Evidence, Location Recovered, Recovered By, and Time. The list of items included:

- Cambridge filter cigarette butt
- Cigarette butt, filter cigarette butt, brand name not listed
- Marlboro filter cigarette butt
- Long brown hair in color
- Long brown hair in color
- Part of the digestive system, it appeared to be intestine
- Part of the digestive system
- Cambridge filter cigarette butt
- Mountain Dew soda pop can, 12 ounce size
- White paper napkin or paper
- White paper x 4
- Soil and leaves and pine needles, trace evidence x 9
- Control sample of soil
- Dark stained soil, leaves, pine needles
- Soil, leaves, pine needles x 4
- Control Dirt Sample
- Control Dirt Sample

As I finished reading the report, my cell buzzed, alerting me to a text message from Amy Smith, one of our team members. "She's back," Amy wrote.

I took a deep breath and asked, "Who is back?"

"See for yourself," Amy answered.

Before I had time to respond, a third text came through. This time, Amy sent a screenshot of a message that read "Charles Ray Vines killed Melissa Witt and I can prove it!"

"Rider," I said, never looking up from my phone. "You… you've got to see this," I stammered.

The retired detective rose from his seat and reached across the table for my phone.

"Here we go again," I sighed as he perused the message..

"Well, I'll be damned," Rider laughed. "Sandy Jones just can't stay away, now can she?"

Chapter 5: Rush to Judgment

I was first contacted by the woman I will refer to as "Sandy Jones" via email in 2016. At the time, Sandy portrayed herself as a close friend of Melissa Witt. It didn't take long, however, for me to realize that Sandy had never been close friends with the 19-year-old college student. Instead, Sandy's only contact with the teenager was as a patient at the dental clinic where Melissa was employed. In fact, Sandy's claims about her relationship with Melissa turned out to be completely false. At best, the two women were no more than casual acquaintances. When confronted with the truth, Sandy's story conveniently shifted. This time, she claimed that, in the weeks leading up to Melissa's death, the young woman had confided in her about a secret romance. "Please don't tell anyone," Melissa allegedly whispered to Sandy. "No one can ever find out."

Determined to get to the bottom of her story, I tracked down one of Sandy's estranged family members. As we sat down for coffee one afternoon, the woman assured me that Sandy's stories about her interaction with Melissa were complete lies. "I care about her," she insisted, "but I keep my distance. She is notorious for gross exaggerations, tall tales, and, sometimes, outright lies."

"Oh boy," I responded with disgust.

"That's not all," she warned. "She is incredibly vindictive. Please be careful."

It's hard to believe, but when I first met Sandy Jones, I truly enjoyed our conversations. Like me, she has a deep passion for true crime, and that, combined with her vast knowledge about dozens of Arkansas cold cases, added intrigue to our discussions. However, the more we talked, a disturbing pattern emerged: Sandy, desperate for recognition and importance, would create outlandish stories about unsolved crimes she claimed she was on the verge of solving. The truth is that she has no professional training, experience, or even the ability to solve a cold case. But despite that reality, Sandy's stories, like a leaky faucet, dripped into the community ever so slowly with each lie she told.

When Sandy first hinted to me that she had "important information" in the Witt case, I wanted to believe her. But her repeated insistence that Melissa's murder centered around a strange cast of characters involved in a large-scale conspiracy to cover up the crime made me suspicious. By the time she alleged that Melissa's death was the result of high stakes gambling, a prominent local businessman, corrupt public officials, and a missing child from Alma, Arkansas, I knew I had to cut ties.

My rejection of Sandy's fabricated story created a drastic shift in her attitude and behavior. In fact, during one of our last conversations, she angrily accused me of playing a role in the "cover up" she claimed was happening in the Witt investigation. To make matters worse, in her anger, she also chose to embark on a maniacal tirade against me that lasted almost ten months. Fortunately for me, her misguided attempt to discredit me personally and professionally failed miserably.

Then, just as quickly as she had appeared in my life, Sandy Jones vanished. For the next twelve months, she was eerily quiet. I was thankful for the reprieve from her drama, but I lived in constant fear that she would one day return.

Unfortunately, it turns out, my concerns were justified. She just couldn't help herself. And on one cloudy August morning, the cunning and calculated Sandy Jones suddenly resurfaced with a new story. This time, she insisted Melissa had been abducted by drug dealers in Fort Coffee, Oklahoma. Her latest yarn included grisly details about Melissa's abduction and murder that had little resemblance to truth. When pressed for details to back up her outlandish claims, Sandy insisted that a retired State Trooper had evidence that pointed to Fort Coffee and that, together, they were days away from "breaking the case wide open." Her ignorance to the facts of the case, combined with a lack of empathy for the emotional and psychological damage she inflicted on Melissa's friends and family was appalling. Her ability to fabricate stories and twist facts to suit her strange agenda was so successful that, at times, even law enforcement officials found it impossible to decipher the truth.

However, she never fooled Jay C. Rider or Chris Boyd. The two seasoned detectives saw right through Sandy's desperate desire to inject turmoil and confusion into the Witt case. Rider and Boyd were instrumental in investigating the Fort Coffee leads in Melissa's case, so they knew, without a doubt, that Sandy Jones was once again lying.

Just days after Melissa disappeared from the Bowling World parking lot, law enforcement, in partnership with the local media, made a plea to the public for information. Anyone who had been to Bowling World on the evening of Thursday, December 1, 1994 was asked to call the Fort Smith Police Department. After the broadcast, the phone rang off the hook. One caller, then another, claimed that around 6:30pm on Thursday, December 1, they had witnessed a white female matching the description of Melissa Ann Witt arguing with an African American male.

A composite sketch was drawn and released to the media. Incredibly, almost overnight, the story took on a life of its own. It began with whispers of drug dealers, Fort Coffee, and unpaid drug debts. Eventually those rumors morphed into tales of Melissa leading a secret life revolving around methamphetamines, sex, and shady characters. These wild and unfounded accusations fueled the already tenuous lines of racial, religious, and socio-economic division in Fort Smith and the surrounding communities.

In 1994, Fort Coffee, a small, almost entirely black community in Oklahoma, was the place to go to buy methamphetamines. And while it was unlikely that Melissa would have any ties to this dangerous community, law enforcement did the only thing they could do: They combed Fort Coffee interviewing witnesses, searching homes, even kicking in doors, on a desperate hunt to find Melissa Witt. The extensive search turned up absolutely nothing that connected Melissa to the dangerous and illegal underbelly of Fort Coffee, Oklahoma.

When the medical examiner's findings were released, the toxicology report also supported the work of investigators: "No drugs were found in her system." After a thorough investigation into the Fort Coffee rumors, and with no trace of drugs in Melissa's system, law enforcement confidently ruled out this scenario.

Despite evidence to the contrary, the Fort Coffee rumors have managed to become legend in the Witt case, with each generation passing down its own version of what "really" happened to Melissa Witt. And now, after almost thirty years, Sandy Jones was trying to fan the flames of a story that only served to damage the Witt case and hurt Melissa's friends and family.

To combat Sandy's foolish efforts to derail the case, our team launched a full-scale social media campaign to educate the community on the facts of Melissa's unsolved murder and to squelch the rumors surrounding Fort Coffee. We considered our efforts a success the day Sandy removed dozens of Facebook posts chock-full of false information about Fort Coffee. And then, just as she has done in the past, Sandy disappeared.

Any hope that Sandy would not resurface again died the afternoon I received a phone call from a local television reporter. "You are never going to believe this, LaDonna," she started off. "But I've received a tip that three different law enforcement agencies, including the FBI, are actively trying to prove that Charles Ray Vines killed Melissa Witt."

I stood in stunned silence.

Charles Ray Vines, also known as the River Valley Killer, now deceased, served life without parole in the Arkansas Department of Correction for murdering Ruth Henderson of Crawford County in 1995 and Juanita Wofford of Fort Smith in 1993. Law enforcement linked Vines to the murders after he was caught raping a 16-year-old Crawford County girl in 2000. According to Jay C. Rider, Vines also admitted to raping an elderly Fort Smith woman in 1993, months before he raped and killed Juanita Wofford. As part of his confession, Vines admitted to having sex with his victims once they were dead. It was reported he told one officer, "That's my favorite kind of sex... the kind with dead women. It's what I fantasize about."

According to Rider, most people in the community respected Vines and thought he was a good person. "The crazy thing about all of this," Rider had told me, "is that Vines seemed normal. People described him as being the best neighbor and an all-around great guy. Most everyone he knew had great things to say about him. They had no idea he was a monster." When Vines was arrested for the attempted rape of the young teenager, DNA evidence from that crime scene was a perfect match for DNA in the murder cases. "It was a relief we caught the guy," Rider explained. "There is just no telling who else he might have hurt or killed."

Eventually, Vines was questioned about his involvement in other crimes, including the murder of Melissa Witt. "I spent five days, eight hours at a time, with Vines," Rider had told me. "He talked about some horrible things he had done. But he was adamant that he didn't kill Melissa."

That day, I stood frozen in place, my phone pressed firmly against my ear. The voice on the other end, loud and pleading, interrupted my thoughts of Charles Vines and Melissa Witt. "LaDonna, are you there? Hello?" the reporter said.

"Oh I'm sorry," I said. "I'm just shocked." After another long pause I asked, "What makes them think it was definitely Vines that killed Melissa?"

"Well, that's where the story gets really wild. A local woman claims she has evidence that links Vines to Witt's murder," she explained.

I gasped. "Do you happen to know her name?" I asked. "Is that something you can share with me?"

"Of course. Her name is Sandy Jones," she responded.

At the sound of Sandy's name, my eyes widened with surprise and my mouth dropped open. As shock and disbelief washed over my body, my phone dropped from my hand, disconnecting our call.

Seconds later, my phone rang again. The reporter opened the call with, "I take it you know Sandy Jones."

"I do know her," I answered slowly. "Can you tell me if she has evidence to support her claims?" I asked.

"Let me check with my source. I'll call you back," she assured.

I hung up the phone and sat down at my desk. It's no secret that the horrific crimes Charles Ray Vines committed have garnered widespread attention and interest. People in Fort Smith have long debated his possible connection to the Witt murder. His status as a violent serial killer has kept him on the forefront as an "interesting possibility" in numerous cold cases. However, many seem to forget one crucial detail: his preferred victim type—elderly women.

According to experts, most serial killers, like Vines, actually have a fantasy "type" or ideal victim. Usually, a killer chooses his victims based on race, gender, physical characteristics, age, or some other specific quality. In reality, a killer is rarely going to find a victim that meets all of the exact qualifications, so they generally seek out people with similar traits.

Because Vines was caught inside a 16-year-old girl's home brutally beating, stabbing, and attempting to rape her, and because she was close in age to Melissa Witt, many have concluded that Vines could be the one responsible for Melissa's murder. However, the perception of this crime, according to Jay C. Rider, is grossly misunderstood. During those long hours that Rider interviewed Vines after his arrest, the serial killer revealed the sequence of events that occurred the day of the attack. When Vines set his sinister plan into motion and broke into that house, his actual target was the young girl's much older mother. Once he was inside, however, there was no going back. It was too late. His rational thoughts, replaced by a blinding and uncontrollable thirst for death, drove him onward, regardless of her age.

It's also important to understand the details of Melissa's murder before jumping to conclusions that Vines was involved. First, consider the medical examiner's report in the Witt case. Melissa's official cause of death was ruled "asphyxiation by strangulation." The report also describes how the leaves and soil found in Melissa's airway indicated she had been strangled face down and that she inhaled debris from the forest floor as she fought for her life. The medical examiner's report also provided other important information: Melissa had non-fatal trauma on the side of her head that was believed to have been caused by a blow or a fall. Additionally, the autopsy indicated Melissa had damage to her larynx as well as a fractured hyoid caused by strangulation. And according to the autopsy, Melissa had not sustained any broken bones or lacerations that would indicate she had been severely beaten prior to her death.

These facts are important when you consider the type of crimes Charles Vines committed. According to Jay. C. Rider, the crimes Vines committed were among some of the most violent acts he had ever witnessed in his career. "Charles Vines was ruthless. He often beat his victims beyond recognition. Vines had no regard for human life. He was an absolute monster." Not only that, Vines had an unsettling pattern: Each victim had, in some way, been a part of his life. He lurked beneath the surface of their quiet lives, watching and waiting, as he plotted their demise. His carefully crafted plans never included random attacks in dimly lit parking lots, kidnapping, or strangulation. Instead, Vines chose to break into the homes of his victims, often kicking in their doors, before unleashing the most sinister and unholy acts of violence that the town of Fort Smith, Arkansas would ever see.

Additionally, Vines, even after being sentenced to consecutive life sentences, adamantly denied his involvement in Melissa's murder. But that's not all. Vines was extensively interviewed by law enforcement, specifically by Jay C. Rider, who, after interviewing the serial killer for over 40 hours, determined there was no connection to Vines and Melissa Witt in life or in death. And when you take Rider's expert opinion, combined with the FBI assessment that Vines did not fit the profile of Melissa's killer, then consider that there is absolutely no credible evidence that points to his involvement in Melissa's murder, the conclusion is simple: Vines is not a viable suspect in the murder of Melisssa Ann Witt.

And yet, Sandy Jones, a menace to cold cases far and wide, was back in action trying to sell her latest theory in the Witt case with no knowledge of her case and no factual information to back up her claims. Incensed, I made some phone calls. First to the Fort Smith Police Department, and then to one of my contacts at the FBI. To my dismay, Sandy's "information" regarding Vines had been enough to spark interest with both agencies. "It warrants further investigation," one officer explained.

"It's certainly interesting," another offered up.

"She's convincing. I'll give her that," the last agent I spoke to said. "But right now, none of the allegations can be substantiated."

"And it's unlikely they will ever be substantiated," I retorted. "This is nothing more than Sandy's way of interjecting herself into the Witt investigation again."

"And that's the very reason we should thoroughly investigate it, so we can cover all of our bases. If Sandy has indeed lied to us, we will deal with that in due time," the officer assured.

"One more thing," I added. "Before we hang up, can you do me a favor?" I asked.

"Of course," he replied. "What's up?"

"Please check Witt's case file. In it, you will find a statement Sandy made to an investigator on the case a few years back regarding the person she, at the time, believed was responsible for both Melissa's murder and the abduction of Morgan Nick from Alma, Arkansas."

The officer's stunned silence was palpable.

"You are about to find out the hard way that Sandy Jones is not credible. In fact, Vines is the fourth person she has tried to pin Witt's murder on," I explained. "And in every scenario, she swears she has undeniable proof of their guilt. Plain and simple: Sandy Jones is a con artist."

As soon as I pressed the button to end our call, my cell phone rang again. This time, it was Jay C. Rider. I answered with "Any updates?"

Not one for small talk either, Rider immediately replied with, "It's official. The FBI and the Fort Smith PD are going to spend time and resources on the Vines angle."

"All because of Sandy Jones?" I asked.

"The short answer is yes. She's been very convincing this go-round," he answered.

"What a rush to judgment," I barked.

"Let's just sit back and see what happens," Rider suggested. "If on the slightest of chances this information is correct, we need it to be fully investigated. We owe it to Melissa."

I knew Rider was right. Activity, even if it doesn't lead to resolution, is important in a case that has sat cold for a long period of time. Like it or not, as the case ages, so do the evidence and all of the people involved with it, such as any witnesses, and even the killer himself. Maybe this new angle of investigation in Melissa's unsolved murder, despite its very low probability of contributing to anything significant in the case, could stir up critical new information.

And while I understand Sandy's fascination with the mystery that has haunted the town of Fort Smith for decades now, there is no doubt that her bizarre and erratic behavior has been detrimental. Her false tips, while frustrating, do, however, serve a purpose. They remind me of the human aspect of this work, and that none of us are immune to the emotional and psychological impact that cases like this have on the human psyche. Despite my frustration with Sandy and her antics, she has become a symbol of the unresolved mysteries we all carry within us—echoes of our own personal trauma that sometimes manifest in unexpected ways.

It's my hope that Sandy's actions, while misleading, might actually inadvertently steer investigators in the right direction. After all, truth often hides in the shadows, waiting for the light of persistence and chance to reveal it.

Chapter 6: The Lineup

The brutal murder of Melissa Witt in 1995 sent shockwaves through Fort Smith, Arkansas. The picturesque town where neighbors knew each other's names and children played freely in the streets was shattered. As the city mourned, Jay C. Rider, Chris Boyd, and a team of seasoned detectives launched a full-scale investigation into the teenager's homicide. In their unyielding pursuit of justice, they found themselves knee-deep in one of the most perplexing murder cases of their careers.

The first few months included a flurry of activity: the crime scene was meticulously combed for evidence, hundreds of people were interviewed, and Melissa's friends and family were scrutinized. As lead after lead was exhausted and the weeks slowly turned into months, and months into years, the trail eventually grew cold.

And then, after four years of silence and mystery, a promising new lead developed. A rookie reporter named Marcus Blair came across significant information while working the police and fire beat for the *Times Record* in Fort Smith. As Blair and his supervisor sat in the newsroom thumbing through various newspapers, they stumbled upon front page news out of Houston, Texas.

A man named Larry Swearingen had been arrested for the murder of a young college student named Melissa Trotter. Swearingen was accused of strangling the 19-year-old young woman to death and dumping her body in the Sam Houston National Forest.

Immediately, Blair noticed similarities between the murder of Melissa Trotter and Melissa Witt. Both women had the same first name and looked similar in physical appearance. Both young women had been abducted, strangled, and their bodies found in a national forest. But what struck Blair the most was the eerie realization that Trotter and Witt were abducted four years apart to the week.

At the urging of his supervisor, Blair immediately contacted the Fort Smith Police Department and scheduled a meeting with Jay C. Rider. By the time the meeting was over, investigators had their eyes set on a promising new lead: Larry Ray Swearingen.

As investigators dug into the new lead, it became clear that the similarities in the Witt and Trotter cases were too many and too striking for them to ignore. Like Blair, law enforcement discovered that both young women shared the same first name, appearance, and build, and both wore similar clothing at the time of their abductions. Both were found by hunters on National Forest land about 50 miles from their abduction sites. They were each missing similar personal effects and both had been strangled.

A thorough investigation into Swearingen would lead Detective Rider to information that would set the Witt case on fire. Rider discovered that Larry Swearingen had been in Arkansas just days before Melissa's murder, visiting his grandparents in Clinton. While there, Swearingen purchased a part for his car. Detective Rider drove to Clinton and tracked down a copy of the receipt. The receipt was not enough to tie Swearingen, even circumstantially, to the crime. However, the receipt, the similarities between the Trotter and Witt murders, and Swearingen's presence in Arkansas days before Witt's death, combined with another strange turn of events, did, according to Rider, make Swearingen a suspect.

That strange turn of events occurred shortly after Rider retired from the Fort Smith Police Department to become the Chief of Police in Barling, Arkansas. One afternoon, Rider received a call from the Texas Attorney General's office. On the call, Rider learned that during a routine cell check on death row, guards found paperwork under his mattress in Swearingen's own handwriting that listed out Rider's name, Melissa's name, and the date December 1, 1994. This information contributed to the cloud of suspicion surrounding Swearingen, but there was still no concrete evidence connecting him to Melissa Witt or Fort Smith, Arkansas.

Despite that, what authorities learned next about Swearingen is chilling. They discovered that when he kidnapped, raped, and murdered Melissa Trotter, he was already under indictment for the kidnapping and sexual assault of his former fiancé. But that's not all. In 1992, Swearingen was convicted of shooting at and kidnapping his wife and sexually assaulting her at a remote location in the woods off Airport Road in Montgomery County, Texas. Later, during the punishment phase of his trial, a former neighbor testified that Swearingen broke into her house, rummaged through her lingerie, and cut off the legs of a pair of pantyhose. His intent? We can only assume it was malicious.

In 1994, the same year that Melissa was murdered, Swearingen tied up, gagged, and sexually assaulted a young female after forcing her to don pantyhose from which the crotch had been removed. And in 1997, Swearingen choked his nine-month-pregnant wife nearly to the point of unconsciousness after accusing her of being unfaithful. Then, in August 1998, he handcuffed, choked, and sexually assaulted his former fiancé. One month later, in September 1998, Swearingen again abducted his former fiancé at gunpoint and forced her to drive to a remote dirt road in the Sam Houston National Forest before releasing her.

So it's no surprise to me that a jury eventually found Swearingen guilty of capital murder and also found there was a probability that he would commit further criminal acts of violence that would constitute a continuing threat to society. There is no doubt that Larry Swearingen was an incredibly dangerous man. But did he kill Melissa Witt? While that question remains unanswered, what we do know is this: Swearingen was convicted and executed for an almost identical crime—the murder of Melissa Trotter. And without a doubt, the Trotter and Witt's cases do mirror each other, so it's not a stretch of the imagination to believe that both murders could have been the work of Larry Swearingen. Until there is evidence to completely rule him out, he will remain a top suspect in Melissa's murder.

Of course, outside of Swearingen, there are also almost a dozen other murderers and rapists who were closely scrutinized in the Witt case. Men such as Charles Ray Vines, Travis Crouch, Douglas Logan, William Dillard Taylor, Jonathan Keith Cole, Harold Solomon and Larry Landrum. However, that shady cast of characters, despite their motives and their secrets, pale in comparison to the *unnamed suspect*.

His name, never released to the public by law enforcement, is embedded inside the pages of Melissa Witt's diary like an elusive clue waiting to unravel the truth behind the teenager's untimely demise.

As police combed through the pages of her diary, they uncovered the turbulent history of Melissa and the unnamed suspect's relationship. Once a seemingly picture-perfect kinship, the connection soured, leaving a trail of emotional turmoil. According to Melissa's diary, the unnamed suspect's behavior, once charming and affectionate, had grown dark and brooding.

His life, police would later learn, embodied the very characteristics assigned to Melisa Witt's killer by the FBI profiler: A hot-tempered, narcissistic, womanizing outdoorsman with little regard for human life.

As I write this chapter, I wrestle with the possibility that I could be veering dangerously close to the edge of sensitive information that has never been publicly disclosed. After all, for many years, naming, or even hinting to the identity of an uncharged suspect was considered problematic for various reasons: First, the concept of "innocent until proven guilty," if ignored, could result in legal implications, including defamation claims. Additionally, revealing a suspect's identity prematurely could compromise a case, as well as impact the person's right to a fair trial.

Over the years, however, there has been a shift in attitude regarding the release of names of suspects in unsolved crimes. Take for instance Richard Jewell. The media identified the security guard as a suspect in the 1996 Centennial Olympic Park Bombing in Atlanta, Georgia. Turns out, Jewell was innocent. And sadly, the disclosure of his name to the press ruined his life.

As I reflect on the fragility of Melissa's unsolved murder case, it is clear that releasing this man's name would be a grave mistake. However, I do believe there are compelling reasons to make the public aware of his existence. First and foremost, I believe he is a credible threat to society. His life, both before and after Melissa's death, is rife with a violent disdain for women. It's critical to share at least some small details about him in hopes it might encourage others to come forward. After all, the man that killed Melissa Witt is not a no-name, fleeting shadowy phantom that vanished into thin air after committing murder. Instead, Melissa's killer is a mere human—a flesh and blood symbol of the darkness that lies hidden in the human heart.

What I do know about the unnamed suspect is that he is a man of considerable charm and intellect. He wields those traits, along with his handsome face and killer smile, like a weapon. Beneath this veneer, however, is a cruel, cold, calculating murderer, devoid of empathy.

His malevolence is painstakingly deliberate. He takes pleasure in the act of manipulation, and relishes in the art of deceit. The depths of his evil, I believe, are most evident in his lack of remorse. He views his victims as expendable chess pieces in a game that he plays with a sadist's joy.

As fate would have it, in 2015, just as *his* desperation for information in Melissa's murder investigation came to a fever-pitch, the *Times Record* ran a story about my documentary team's pursuit for answers in the Witt case. Consumed by his obsession with Melissa Witt, he made a decision that changed both of our lives: he called me.

This unnamed suspect first made contact with me around 1:00 a.m. on a Wednesday morning. When I answered the phone, I was greeted by the muffled sounds of a man sobbing.

"Hello?" I answered.

"Is this…" he hesitated. "Is this LaDonna? The woman from the newspaper article?" he asked.

Stunned, I sat straight up in my bed, waking my husband in the process. "How did you get this number?" I demanded.

"I just can't believe she's dead," he cried. "I don't want her to be dead."

Perplexed, I asked, "Who is dead? Why are you calling me?"

"Melissa Witt," he said through gritted teeth. "Melissa is dead. She is dead dead."

I sat in stunned silence.

"Will you take me to her grave?" he asked. "I want to say goodbye properly this time."

As my heart raced, I motioned for my husband to grab some paper and a pencil. "Of course I will take you to Melissa's grave," I assured. "Let's both get some rest and I will call you tomorrow so we can make a plan on where to meet up. Can I have your name? Your phone number?"

As I scrawled his name across the page of my spiral-bound notebook, I had no way of knowing that exactly 21 years earlier, Melissa, too, had penned this very name within the pages of her own small spiral-bound notebook.

Today, if we were to lay those notebooks side by side, each would hold vastly different secrets within their covers. The first, a diary belonging to a teenage girl with dreams as numerous as the stars. The diary was Melissa's confidant, a silent keeper of her innermost thoughts. Her innocent musings about this man included: "He is a very sweet guy."

Beside it, the second notebook, would be a stark contrast of methodical, meticulously maintained notes regarding the murder investigation of a teenage girl. The pages, filled with observations, hunches, facts, and evidence of a crime that had shaken the community. My description of the same man, however, was in vast opposition to Melissa's. "He is manipulative and violent. Is he the killer?" I wrote.

Only one of us could be right.

Chapter 7: Dancing with the Devil

I sat anxiously in the dimly lit corner of the Embassy Suites hotel bar. The buzz of conversation and clinking glasses provided a fitting backdrop for a covert meeting with an informant in the Witt case. Three days earlier, I'd received a one-sentence email from him that captured my attention: "Probably not relevant, but my old college roommate told me he was meeting Melissa Witt the night she disappeared." As fate would have it, this informant had been the roommate of the man who called me in the middle of the night just days before.

My eyes scanned the tapestry of bar patrons: business travelers sipping scotch, couples laughing over a glass of wine, and a group of friends recounting their day's adventures over shared appetizers. I paused on each face, searching for the author of the email.

A few minutes later, a tall figure approached, his face obscured by the brim of a hat. "LaDonna?" his voice was low, just above a whisper. I nodded, my heart racing, "I'm Nixon," he announced.

He removed his hat and sat down at our secluded table. As the ambient lighting cast shadows over our tense expressions, Nixon slid an envelope across the table. "It's all in there. Everything he ever told me about Melissa Witt."

I opened the envelope and pulled out a single piece of paper. Written on it was a name—one that I had seen before in Melissa Witt's diary. My eyes widened in shock; the man named on this paper was our unnamed suspect.

"Are you sure about this?" I asked, my mind racing.

Nixon leaned closer, his eyes darting around the room. "Absolutely. But there's more. He also kept a Mickey Mouse watch on display in our apartment."

My breath caught in my throat. "He kept a Mickey Mouse watch?"

Nixon hesitated, his voice dropping even lower. "What if it's Melissa's watch?"

Fear and disbelief gripped my heart. Nixon was not just a detached bystander; he was intimately connected to the suspect.

"Did he tell you that he's been calling me?" I asked.

The color drained from Nixon's face as he absorbed my question. "You've been talking to *him*?" Nixon asked, his voice tinged with concern and disbelief.

I nodded solemnly while a heavy silence settled over the table as we both considered the gravity of the situation. With fear slowly easing its way into my mind, the once-buzzing atmosphere of the bar suddenly felt oppressive. What if Nixon had arranged this meeting to lure me into a trap? What if the unnamed suspect was lurking in the shadows?

Without warning, Nixon rose to his feet. "Be careful, LaDonna," he cautioned. "He can't ever find out we have spoken. He's more dangerous than you can ever imagine." And with that, Nixon O'Neil disappeared into the crowd, leaving me alone with information that, if true, held the power to change everything in the Witt case.

I glanced around the room, forming a strategy to exit safely, then stood to leave. I decided to avoid the main entrance and headed toward the back door instead. As I walked, I pulled out my phone to call Jay. C. Rider.

I could feel eyes on me as I made my way through the maze of tables toward the back entrance of the bar. My heart was pounding as I reached for the door, pushed it open, and stepped into the cool night air.

I quickly made my way to my car while constantly looking over my shoulder. Once locked inside my Suburban, I left a message for Rider. "Listen, I've got something that could be big. Please call me."

Seconds later, my phone rang.

"Rider," I said, my voice a mixture of excitement and urgency. "I just came from a meeting with a man who has some information on the unnamed suspect."

I glanced around the parking lot before I continued. "The informant, Nixon O'Neil, was in the suspect's inner circle. They even lived together in college. But that's not all, he also shared something even more explosive. He claims the suspect kept a Mickey Mouse Watch on display in their apartment."

The retired detective's voice was slow and steady, yet I could sense his excitement and concern. "LaDonna, where are you? Where did you meet Nixon?"

"Outside the hotel bar at Embassy Suites," I replied hesitantly.

Rider, understanding the gravity of the situation at hand, demanded I leave. "Get out of there, but don't go straight home. Make sure he's not following you. I will be in touch soon. Be careful, LaDonna You're playing with fire here."

I gripped the steering wheel tightly as I drove toward home, replaying the meeting at the hotel bar over and over in my mind. There was a raw sincerity in Nixon's voice, an urgency that suggested he genuinely wanted Melissa's case to be solved. My gut told me that, despite the risks and uncertainties associated with an informant like Nixon, I could trust him.

Moments later, as I drove down the highway, the flashing lights of a passing police car interrupted my thoughts and snapped me back into reality. While I was mentally rehashing events from earlier in the evening, I had driven past my exit. Realizing my mistake, I took a deep breath, turned my car around, and circled back toward home.

As I approached my house, I could see my children through the living room window, and a sense of dread settled over me. The Witt case had now become different, more personal. The unnamed suspect was not just a name in a file. He was a real person. A dangerous individual with a new hobby—contacting me.

The next morning, I grappled with a difficult decision—to abandon my work in the Witt investigation for the sake of my family or to press on in my pursuit for justice. In my heart, I knew I couldn't turn away from Melissa's case. Inexplicably, the looming threat of the unnamed suspect not only did not deter me, it served as fuel for my desire to find justice for a girl I never knew. So I did what I could and took precautions to safeguard my family.

Late nights turned into early mornings as I chased leads, interviewed witnesses, scrutinized every piece of information with meticulous detail, and spent countless hours discreetly learning as much as I could from the unnamed suspect about his life and his relationship with Melissa. I immersed myself in his world, letting the threads of friendship weave themselves naturally while maintaining the delicate balance between gaining his trust and not arousing suspicion.

As the days turned into weeks, my rapport with this man deepened. I learned about his troubled past, his struggles, and the demons that haunted him. All the while, I remained vigilant, searching for any hints or clues that might tie him to Melissa's murder.

He shared with me his greatest joys and fears and his deepest regrets. At times, I wrestled with conflicting emotions—empathy for the deeply troubled person I was getting to know and a burning rage and disgust at the thought of his possible involvement in Melissa's murder.

Eventually, during one of our late-night phone calls, he revealed a chilling detail that sent shivers down my spine. "She told me she would be at Bowling World that night," he explained.

My heart stopped.

"Did you go…" I paused. "Did you go to Bowling World that night to meet her?"

"I would have married her," he answered. "She was such a sweet, sweet girl."

I sat in silence and seethed.

"She didn't deserve to be raped and murdered," he whispered.

His words became a trigger, unlocking the buried memories of the crime scene photos taken in the Ozark National Forest of Melissa's lifeless body. My thoughts immediately shifted into overdrive. According to the Medical Examiner's report, it was *impossible* to determine if Melissa had been raped. The gravity of his statement weighed heavily on my heart. Had he genuinely slipped up and given me information only the killer would know? Or was he a master manipulator seeking attention?

"Why do you think she was raped?" I asked.

"She was a virgin," he responded, slurring his words. "She's dead. Oh my god, she's dead," he cried. Then he hung up.

Overwhelmed, I sat down at my kitchen table and wept.

The next morning, with the emotional turmoil of my undercover mission still weighing heavily on me, I decided to take a break from the unnamed suspect. I pushed him from the recesses of my mind and focused on the day ahead. It was a typical Monday. I made breakfast, dropped the kids off at school and daycare, grabbed my morning coffee from the Starbucks drive-thru, and ventured on to my job as a sober living director. As I walked inside the office that morning, my assistant, Cindy, gave me a knowing look.

"Good morning, LaDonna!" she offered cheerily. "I left a *few* things on your desk."

"Morning," I shouted as I rounded the corner to my office. *Just a few things?* I thought to myself as I pushed the door open. My jaw dropped as I glanced inside the cramped room. My desk was covered with a mountain of paperwork. Drug screen results, mail, court requests, applications, and discharge reports demanded my immediate attention. Glancing at my watch, I slumped into my black leather office chair. "Cindy," I called out wearily. "I'm not taking any walk-in appointments today, okay?"

Moments later, Cindy cautiously peered into my office and smiled. "Got it," she said as she pointed to the tower of paperwork. "More coffee?"

"Please," I answered dully as I dove into the sea of paperwork. Minutes later, Cindy returned with a steaming cup of java.

"Thank you… so much," I offered between sips as Cindy plopped down in the worn-out chair across from me.

"I know you aren't taking walk-in appointments," she started off. "*But* there is a woman waiting out front to see you. She just arrived and she seems very distraught."

I raised my eyebrows as I thumbed through the large pile on my desk. "Okay, send her in," I sighed. As Cindy left to retrieve the woman from the lobby, I gulped down half of my coffee. I made a lame attempt at restacking the papers on my desk more neatly and stood just as Cindy guided a well-dressed woman into my office. "Hi, LaDonna," she said as I stood to greet her. "Thank you for seeing me today."

"Of course," I answered as I leaned across my desk to shake her hand. "How can I help you?" I asked.

Cindy gently closed my office door behind her as I settled back into my chair. My guest took a seat and forced a smile as she pointed at my desk. "Should I come back another time?"

I chuckled. "To be honest, I would rather meet with you than wade through this mess," I said. The woman looked away nervously before making eye contact again. When our eyes finally met, her tear-stained face told a story: This woman was suffering under the weight of pain and fear.

"What can I help you with today?" I asked. "Are you or a family member struggling with a drug addiction?"

"No!" she half-yelled in response. "No, it's nothing like that. I am here for a different reason. I need to…" her voice trailed off.

"Okay… can you tell me why you are so upset?" I asked gently.

"I'm here to discuss the Melissa Witt case," she whispered. She looked down at her well-manicured hands.

"I am sorry to show up here... like this... but I wanted to meet with you in person."

Frustrated, I leaned back in my chair and folded my arms across my chest. "I'm very sorry," I said firmly, "but I don't want to mix my work on the Witt case with my full-time job. I'm here to help women recover from drugs and alcohol. I hope you understand."

Tears flowed down the woman's face as she quickly rose from her seat. "I'm so sorry," she cried. "It's just that I was in the parking lot the night Melissa was abducted. I overheard their argument!"

I relaxed my arms and leaned forward. "Please sit back down," I urged. "Please."

"I'm terrified!" she blurted out. "What if he finds out who I am and tries to kill me?" she asked through frightened tears. Instinctively, I reached for the box of Kleenex perched at the far corner of my desk. As I strained to reach the tissue, I knocked over my ceramic coffee mug. As the remaining hot liquid rushed over the surface of my desk, the woman fell back into the worn-out visitor's chair and wept.

"It's going to be okay," I assured her as I reached for a roll of paper towels on the filing cabinet behind my desk. As I soaked up the large brown puddle, the woman continued to sob. "I was walking back to my car that night in the Bowling World parking lot," she explained. "I could hear them fighting... Melissa and the man who killed her. I can still remember the sound of his voice."

Despite my racing heart, I remained calm as I tossed the wet paper towels in the trash can near my desk and sat back down. "Could you hear what they were arguing about?" I asked quietly. "Or could you hear Melissa say his name?"

"I remember that his name started with…" she sobbed. "His name started with the letter…"

I struggled to keep my composure the moment the letter of his first name left her lips. I took a deep breath. I couldn't bring myself to tell her that a man whose name is well known to Witt investigators also starts with the same letter.

"I want to do something," she cried. "With some help, I think I could remember more details from that night at Bowling World."

"What kind of help do you think you need?" I asked as our eyes locked.

"I want help remembering his name," she said. "I want to be hypnotized."

Chapter 8: Hypnotized

The tires of my Suburban hummed against the asphalt as I drove from Northwest Arkansas through the winding roads leading to Fort Smith. The crisp autumn air whipped through the open windows, carrying with it a sense of anticipation. I was on my way to witness a pivotal moment in the investigation into Melissa's unsolved murder—a woman being hypnotized in hopes of unlocking the secrets hidden deep within her memories.

As I pulled into the parking lot of our meeting location—a local hotel—my heart rate quickened. Inside, a hypnotist rumored to have a gift for uncovering buried memories awaited, along with Carol Johnson, the woman who had been present at the scene of Melissa's abduction in the Bowling World parking lot. Her life, forever changed by that chance encounter on that fateful December night in 1994, has been plagued with a gnawing sense of guilt—she blames herself for the series of events that ultimately resulted in Melissa's brutal murder.

"I wish I could have somehow stopped the argument in the parking lot that night," she shared with me one afternoon. "Sometimes I think this is my fault," her voice trailed off.

"No! No, it isn't!" I interjected immediately. "This was his fault—and his *alone*. The man that killed Melissa is a monster. And I am so thankful he didn't kidnap and kill *two* victims that night," I gently reassured her.

Determined to help ease Carol's emotional turmoil, while also uncovering the truth from her fragmented memories, I worked with retired investigators to set up a session with a hypnotist. While inadmissible in court, hypnosis, like a polygraph, can be a valuable tool in a cold case. The process of hypnosis involves putting a witness in a comfortable, relaxing state that is free of distractions. Experts have discovered that those conditions can often enhance eyewitness recall.

However, there is a downside to hypnosis. It can be very difficult to separate what someone actually remembers and what psychologists call confabulation.

Confabulation involves mistakenly recalling false information without intending to deceive. It can sometimes occur when a witness remembers incorrect information in vivid detail. The selection of a reputable hypnotist who is careful not to introduce information during the session is key to a successful outcome.

It's also important to point out that although courts have almost unanimously ruled that exculpatory statements made under hypnosis are inadmissible, they have consistently allowed witnesses to testify to facts remembered *after* investigatory hypnosis for memory enhancement.

Armed with those facts, Chris Boyd researched, found, and scheduled a credible hypnotist to assist Carol in retrieving critical information from that night in the Bowling World parking lot. Rider and I chose a hotel nestled on the outskirts of Fort Smith as the location for Carol to delve into her memories and unlock the secrets she had carried for almost thirty years.

As night fell and the town slipped into darkness, we found ourselves sitting in the dimly lit confines of a hotel suite. Under hypnosis, Carol dove into her memories with remarkable clarity. The parking lot of the bowling alley flashed before her eyes. She recalled fleeting glimpses of the scene: a dark parking lot barely illuminated by flickering streetlights, an imposing figure arguing with a young woman—figures and faces obscured, and, most importantly, she remembered that his name starts with the letter D.

At Carol's admission, I let out a quiet gasp. The man's name in Melissa's diary—the same man who was Nixon O'Neil's old roommate—the one who had confided in me that Melissa Witt had been raped—his name starts with the letter D.

As the hypnotist guided Carol deeper into the trance-like state, the lines between reality and memory blurred for me. Carol felt herself being drawn back to that fateful night, her senses heightened and the images of the parking lot flooded her consciousness. "Leave me alone," she recalled Melissa yelling at the mysterious man. "Get away from me!"

My eyes filled with tears as I pictured Melissa with her vibrant smile and carefree spirit. Innocent plans to see her mother thwarted by a man lurking in the shadows whose obsession with her had turned toxic and dangerous. As Melissa stepped out into the dimly lit parking lot, and before she could react, he emerged from the darkness, his eyes filled with a twisted mix of longing and rage. They argue and, in a blur of motion, he strikes Melissa on the head, sending her crumpling to the ground in a daze. I imagine his face as he drags Melissa into his car and speeds off into the night, leaving behind a trail of fear and confusion.

As the events of Thursday, December 1, 1994 replayed in my mind, the hypnotist gently guided Carol back to consciousness. She described how the experience of hypnotism had "brought her memories into laser sharp focus." "My memories that once felt fragmented and elusive are now tangible and real," Carol explained as we locked eyes. In that moment I knew that she could very well hold the key to unlocking the truth behind Melissa's murder.

Even though almost thirty years have passed since that chilling night when Melissa Witt disappeared, the revelation brought forth by Carol Johnson has given all of us a new lead to pursue: a name that started with the letter "D."

As I left the hotel that night to head back to Northwest Arkansas, D's name echoed in my mind like a distant whisper. This was the clue we needed to unlock the secrets of the Witt murder. With renewed determination, I combed through the case files once more, searching through the decades-old records for additional traces of information that connected the elusive "D" to Melissa.

Days turned into weeks, but I refused to give up hope. Then, one rainy afternoon, a breakthrough came in the form of an email. In it, a woman detailed out a troublemaker with a history of violence against women—including the author. D's name flashed in my mind, sending a surge of adrenaline coursing through my veins. I responded to the email immediately. My only question: "Was his name D…?"

Minutes later another email hit my inbox: "Can I call you, please?" she asked.

"Yes," I responded, providing her with my phone number.

Seconds later, my phone rang. Her voice, just above a whisper, confirmed my suspicion: "I didn't want to put this in writing," she explained. "But his name is 'D.' Do you know him?"

My blood ran cold.

I knew what I had to do. Setting my fear aside, I embarked on a daring investigation to reach out to all of D's former girlfriends in search of clues that could shed light on his hidden secrets. What I discovered shook me to the core. I uncovered a pattern of abuse and manipulation that stretched back for almost three decades. Each woman I spoke to shared harrowing tales of violence and control, recounting instances where D's charming demeanor gave way to a cruel and sadistic nature.

It was the stories of four women in particular that sent shivers down my spine. All four women had been in relationships with him, and all four had narrowly escaped with their lives after enduring unimaginable horrors at his hands.

As I listened to their accounts, my heart ached with sympathy for the women who had suffered at the hands of a man they had once loved. But it was the chilling similarity between their stories that caught my attention—all four women had been strangled by him, their lives hanging in the balance as he exerted his twisted dominance over them. Unlike Melissa Witt, they had all survived.

With a sinking feeling in the pit of my stomach, I realized that the unnamed suspect's history of violence went far beyond what I had initially suspected. He wasn't just a suspect in a murder case—he was a dangerous predator capable of unspeakable cruelty.

Armed with this newfound knowledge, I pressed on with my investigation, determined to bring him to justice for his heinous crimes. But as I dug deeper, I couldn't shake the feeling that I was treading on dangerous ground, tiptoeing along the edge of a darkness that surrounded a man who was closely monitoring my investigation.

One evening, as I sat in my home office, pouring over notes from research into D's life, the cell phone rang shrilly, shattering the silence of the night. With a sense of dread, I hesitantly picked up my phone, only to be met with a chilling voice on the other end.

"I don't have any secrets you can uncover, LaDonna," the voice sneered, dripping with malice. "You have no idea what you are doing."

His taunt echoed in my ears. It was clear he knew he was being investigated, and he wasn't afraid to let me know it. With each subsequent phone call, he waffled between veiled threats laced with a sadistic glee and a tear-filled conversation that detailed the despair he felt over the loss of Melissa Witt.

Despite the fear that gripped my heart, I refused to back down. I knew that he was dangerous, but my resolve was strengthened by the knowledge that justice demanded nothing less. Over the months, his calls grew more desperate, his attempts to intimidate me failed. And then, one night, the phone rang for the final time. It was him that found himself on the receiving end of a call he never expected.

With trembling hands, I dialed his number. As I waited for him to answer, I felt a surge of adrenaline surge through my veins. I was prepared to confront the man who may hold the key to unlocking the mystery of Melissa Witt's murder.

"Hello?" came the voice on the other end, a tone of cautious curiosity tinged with suspicion.

"D?" I asked, my voice steady despite the emotions that swirled inside my heart.

There was a moment of silence before he responded with a single word.

"Yes?"

Summoning every ounce of courage I possessed, I pressed on, determined to confront him with the question that had been burning in my mind since I first embarked on this journey.

"There is something I need to know," I began, my voice tinged with rage. "Did you do it? Did you kill Melissa Witt?"

There was silence on the other end. The tension was so thick, I could almost feel it pressing down on me like a weight. And then, finally, he spoke, his voice low and chilling.

"I loved her, LaDonna," he said, his voice laced with a quiet menace that frightened me. "Of course," he paused, "I didn't kill her," he sneered

The phone went dead.

I know I'm treading on dangerous ground, playing a high-stakes game with a man who holds the power to either condemn or exonerate himself with his words. And so, armed with nothing but unwavering determination and unyielding resolve, I will continue to pursue the elusive murder suspect whose name starts with the letter D. I refuse to stop until I can finally bring him to justice for all of the lives he has shattered in the wake of his reckless pursuit of power and control over women.

Chapter 9: It's in the Details

Cases like Melissa's go cold for a number of reasons: lack of physical evidence, no witness testimony, or no confession. And in the United States, there are approximately 285,000 cases that have gone cold for those very reasons. Sadly, only one in 5 cold cases will ever identify a new suspect. Of those suspects, only one in 20 will ever get charged and only one in 100 of those charged will ever be convicted.

In many of these cold cases, there are dozens of circumstances, such as red herrings, that distract investigators and send them down the wrong path. Sometimes, even important clues are overlooked. But in the vast majority of these unsolved cases, investigators are simply overwhelmed. It's challenging for law enforcement to handle the sheer volume of horrific crimes that are reported to them on a regular basis. Unfortunately, police simply don't have the time or the patience to investigate each and every crime that is on their radar. It's a vicious cycle, because the lack of time and attention is the largest contributing factor to a case going cold. I have learned over the years that it's imperative to delve into the details of these cases from day one if there is ever going to be any hope of resolution.

Every murder tells a story if you take the time to understand the intricate details surrounding the crime. And those critical details can be found in a variety of places such as crime scene photos, autopsy reports, witness interviews, and embedded within the pages of notes taken by investigators. The original investigation into Melissa's murder, while not perfect, was incredibly thorough. Both Jay C. Rider and Chris Boyd have poured their hearts and souls into this case, chasing down every lead and scrutinizing every piece of evidence in their quest for justice.

But despite their tireless efforts, the truth has remained elusive, taunting them from the shadows like a specter from the past. Melissa's murder has haunted them both for years—a cold and unsolved puzzle that is still waiting to be solved.

And now, decades later, both retired detectives have allowed me to join forces with them to re-examine evidence and bring fresh eyes to the long-forgotten investigation. Due to the complexity of Melissa's case, we have taken a multi-faceted approach. First, we started by reviewing the case files. This has included reading through police reports, witness testimony, and any other documentation related to Melissa's case. This has been incredibly beneficial for me when it comes to understanding the nature of the crime, the evidence that was gathered at the time, and any potential leads that were pursued in the case.

The next step has been to re-interview witnesses. Sometimes talking to witnesses again can provide valuable information that was not uncovered during the initial investigation. This, too, has helped me get a better understanding of what happened, who was involved, and whether there have been any new developments since the crime was originally committed.

Another important step has been re-examining old evidence that was collected right after the crime occurred in 1994. This has included reviewing physical evidence such as fingerprints, hair and fibers, as well as other evidence that may have been overlooked during the initial investigation.

Additionally, we have spent countless hours following up on leads that could be beneficial in solving Melissa's case. This has involved analyzing new evidence as well as conducting surveillance. Both Rider and Boyd have taught me to use a thorough and systematic approach in each of these steps as we review Melissa's case so we might increase our chances of solving her murder once and for all.

We have also successfully utilized social media by posting information about Melissa's case to help generate tips and leads. Social media has also allowed us to reach a wider audience to spread the word that Melissa's murder remains unsolved.

And while the two men find themselves drawn back to the case that has haunted them since their days at the Fort Smith Police Department, their attention has also been focused on the details written by Melissa herself in a small spiral-bound diary. They have carefully examined the pages, their eyes scanning the handwritten entries for any clue that could lead them to Melissa's killer.

With confidence, both men have assured me that the name of the man that murdered Melissa Witt can be found within the pages of the journal that documented the various relationships that were important to her. One moniker in particular caught their attention early on as they searched for any mention of the name that could belong to her killer.

As I studied Melissa's diary closely one morning at the Fort Smith Police Department in 2018, I paid special attention to the entries about the unnamed suspect. *"I talked to 'D' for a minute,"* Melissa wrote in her diary. *"He's supposed to call me back, but we'll see. I'm sitting here waiting on him to call right now. I kept telling myself that I would not allow myself to start doing this. But here I am—just sitting here waiting. He probably won't even call me back tonight. I am so naive and stupid to be doing this. Maybe D isn't the right guy for me to date. Supposedly he wants to date me next year when we're both at UALR, but that probably isn't true either. I am just so confused—I don't know what to believe. I guess we'll just have to see.—Melissa."*

"He's our guy," I whispered to myself as I thought about the growing cloud of suspicion centering on this man. Every piece of the puzzle seems to point to him—his motive, his opportunity, and his temperament. Suddenly, my thoughts were interrupted by the sounds of my cell phone buzzing. A Facebook message from a woman whose name I didn't recognize was sitting in my inbox. Intrigued, I clicked on the message. Her words were short and to the point, containing only a few cryptic sentences: "The man you are looking for dated Melissa Witt. He is a very violent, manipulative person. Please check into him. I also think you should know that at least one other woman has died suspiciously in his presence."

My heart was pounding with anticipation as I hurriedly typed back my reply. "Can you tell me his name?" I asked before hitting send.

She responded immediately and I froze in fear after reading her message. "His name is D…," she responded. "If you want to know more, meet me at the library in Fort Smith tomorrow at noon. Come alone."

As instructed, I arrived at the library just before noon the next day. Inside, I grabbed a seat at a small table and awaited the arrival of the anonymous informant. My anticipation grew as the clock on the wall ticked away the minutes—each one feeling like an eternity. Promptly at noon, an older woman approached my table. My heart quickened as she took a seat opposite me. "I have something you'll want to see," she said as she pushed a folded newspaper in my direction.

I unfolded the paper to reveal an obituary—not for Melissa Witt, but for another young woman who had died mysteriously. As I read through the article, my mind raced with questions. The details surrounding this young woman's passing were shrouded in mystery—a fact that hadn't escaped the woman sitting across the table from me.

"This isn't just a coincidence," she insisted. "There's something more to this than meets the eye. And I think it's connected to the murder of Melissa Witt."

My pulse raced with excitement as I processed the implications of this woman's words. Could this young woman's death hold the key to unlock the truth behind the murder of Melissa Witt?

"That's not all," the woman added as she rose from her chair to leave. "He dated a friend of mine. She told me he was incredibly violent… and she was terrified of him."

"Sadly, I'm not surprised. I've heard these things about him before," I responded. "I believe what you are telling me. And I also believe there is no doubt that he is an incredibly dangerous man."

As I stood to leave, our eyes locked. "He also has a Mickey Mouse watch, LaDonna. My friend saw it on multiple occasions," she stated flatly. "I would bet my life that it's Melissa's watch." And with that, she turned and walked away.

As I hurried out of the library, my mind buzzed with possibilities. My desire to uncover the truth was stronger than ever. Immediately, I delved into the life of the young woman whose name was found in the obituary. The clues and leads I uncovered during that investigation led me down a twisting path of deceit and betrayal that pointed to one man: the unnamed suspect. I met with dozens of friends and family members of the young woman and they each described the horrific abuse she suffered at the hands of the unnamed suspect. "He killed her," one family member boldly proclaimed. "He did it and we will never be able to prove it."

Despite the suspicion and circumstantial evidence surrounding him, my investigation was stymied by a lack of concrete proof. What I did uncover, however, is a disturbing pattern of violence against women, with multiple complaints filed against him over the years. Yet, somehow, he always managed to evade serious consequences, leaving a trail of destruction in his wake.

With the help of my dedicated team, we pieced together the puzzle of the unnamed suspect's life, scouring both the internet and his hometown for any shred of evidence that could tie him to Melissa's murder and other crimes. Days turned into weeks and then into months with no real progress. But then, just when it seemed as though all hope was lost, we received another tip about the unnamed suspect.

The phone rang loudly, breaking my concentration. I glanced at the caller ID, and my curiosity was piqued by the unfamiliar number. With a quick swipe, I answered the call.

"Hello?" I said calmly.

"Is this LaDonna Humphrey?" a frantic voice on the other end asked.

"Yes, this is she. How can I help you?" I replied, leaning forward in my chair.

"My name is Angelique Thompson. I'm calling because I need to tell you something about my ex-boyfriend. I think he's responsible for a house fire that killed two people," she blurted out, her voice trembling with emotion.

My heart skipped a beat at Angelique's words. Her ex-boyfriend, I knew, was our unnamed suspect. "Tell me everything," I urged, my instincts as a journalist kicking into high gear.

She took a deep breath before launching into her story. She explained that on the evening of the fire, both she and the unnamed suspect were at the mutual friend's house. "I waited in the car while he went inside," she explained. "When he came back to the car, he was acting strangely, his eyes wild with excitement. I found out later that after we left, the house erupted in flames, killing everyone inside."

A small gasp slipped from my lips.

"I know him. I know what he's capable of," she continued, her voice filled with conviction. "He's dangerous. And I am afraid he's a cold-blooded killer."

I listened intently, my mind racing with possibilities. If Angelique's story was true, the unnamed suspect could be responsible for multiple murders. I disconnected the call with Angelique and dialed Jay C. Rider. I needed to share my findings with him and devise a plan to bring the unnamed suspect to justice once and for all.

"Hello?" came Rider's voice on the other end of the line, gruff but warm.

"I think the unnamed suspect could be responsible for multiple murders," I responded.

There was a pause on the other end of the line, and then Rider's voice came through, filled with curiosity. "Go on," he urged.

I quickly relayed my findings, detailing my research and presenting the evidence I had uncovered. I explained my theory that the unnamed suspect was a killer who had been operating under the radar for decades.

As I spoke, I could hear the gears turning in Rider's mind. I knew he was considering my words carefully, weighing the evidence and assessing the situation. Then, after a moment of silence, Rider spoke, his voice filled with determination.

"We need to catch him," Rider said firmly. "We owe it to the victims and their families to bring him to justice."

I felt a surge of adrenaline course through my body at Rider's words. I knew the road ahead of us would be long, but with Rider's and Boyd's expertise and my determination, the three of us would never stop until the unnamed suspect is held accountable for his crimes.

We devised a plan—to gather the evidence and information needed to ensure that the unnamed suspect— the man whose name starts with the letter D—never has the opportunity to harm another innocent soul again.

To this day, the three of us—Jay C. Rider, Chris Boyd, and I continue to pursue that plan, undeterred by the challenges and obstacles that stand in our way. It's a dangerous journey, fraught with uncertainty and peril, but one that we are willing to undertake in pursuit of justice for Melissa Witt.

We have spent countless hours poring over old case files, following up on leads, and tracking down witnesses in our relentless pursuit of the truth. Every piece of evidence, every scrap of information brings us closer to unraveling the mystery that has haunted us for so long.

Together, we have weathered setbacks and disappointments, but we refuse to give up hope. We know that our journey is far from over, and that the road ahead will be paved with difficulty, but we also know that we cannot rest. And so, we continue to press forward, drawing strength from each other and the knowledge that our cause is just. There is no turning back. This is a journey worth taking, and we will see it through until we achieve our ultimate goal: justice for Melissa Witt.

Chapter 10: Shadows of the Past

Almost three decades after Melissa Witt's brutal murder, the past resurfaced in a chilling phone call I received one afternoon. As I sat in my office, sifting through old newspaper clippings about the Witt case, my phone rang.

I answered to the voice of a man who sounded as though the weight of the world sat on his shoulders. "My name is Christopher Myers," the caller said. "I need to talk to you about the Melissa Witt murder case."

My heart skipped a beat. "I'm listening," I replied.

Christopher Myers began to recount a chilling tale. According to Christopher, he was an old friend of the unnamed suspect and knew secrets about him that he had never shared with anyone. But, as the years passed, the weight of his silence had become unbearable.

"He took me to the same logging road where they found her body," Christopher revealed, his voice trembling. "I've carried that guilt with me all of these years."

I felt a surge of anticipation mixed with dread. Could Christopher's revelation finally provide the breakthrough the case needed? I urged him to share every detail he could remember.

Christopher took a deep breath, his voice shaking as he continued his account. "When we arrived at the location where Melissa's body had been discovered," he said, his words carrying the weight of years of silence, "he began to weep."

His story sent a shiver down my spine. It was an unexpected and haunting detail. The image of the unnamed suspect, overcome with grief, standing at the very spot where he had left Melissa's lifeless body, was chilling.

"At the time, I didn't know what to think," Christopher explained, his voice cracking with emotion. "I always wondered how he knew the exact location of where her body was found. I should have come forward sooner. I'm sorry that I didn't."

I could sense the guilt and fear that had haunted Christopher for all these years. As a fraternity brother, he felt an unwavering sense of duty to keep the secret. The bonds forged within the fraternity ran deep, and they were built on trust, loyalty, and solidarity. It was a code of silence that transcended individual concerns and personal guilt. Over the years, Christopher grappled with his conscience, wrestling with the moral dilemma of maintaining the silence. Guilt gnawed at him, but every time he considered breaking the code, he thought of the brotherhood's motto: "In unity, strength." It was a reminder that their collective bond was more significant than any Individual's misdeeds.

Now, with the secret revealed, he had opened a door to the past, possibly shedding new light on the circumstances surrounding Melissa Witt's murder.

Christopher's voice cracked as he continued, "I believe he took me to that remote logging road as some sort of silent confession. Why else would he take me there?"

"I'm not sure," I responded.

"I think he killed that girl," Christopher answered. "I think he did it."

The weight of Christopher's story pressed upon me even more heavily as I processed his words. It was a chilling revelation that transformed the already grim narrative into something even darker. The remote logging road, once a haunting crime scene, had now become an ominous warning, a place where the unnamed suspect had demonstrated the power of fear.

The room seemed to grow colder, and a sense of foreboding settled over me. I felt a surge of anger and determination. The darkness that had shrouded this case for thirty years was beginning to lift, and the truth seemed to be emerging, piece by agonizing piece.

If D was responsible for the murder of Melissa Witt, I knew there could be several reasons why he returned to the crime scene. According to the FBI's Behavioral Analysis Unit (BAU) and various criminal profiling studies, offenders, in some cases, may return to the scene of a crime to re-enact or revisit it. This behavior is often driven by complex psychological factors and serves several purposes:

- **Fantasy Reenactment:** Offenders may return to the crime scene to relive the experience or fulfill their fantasies related to the crime. This can provide them with a sense of power and control.
- **Emotional Gratification:** Returning to the scene may evoke strong emotions, such as excitement, fear, or arousal, which the offender may find satisfying or pleasurable.
- **Taunting or Power Play:** Some offenders may return to the crime scene to taunt law enforcement or the public. This can be a way for them to demonstrate their perceived superiority or intelligence.
- **Confusion or Misdirection:** Offenders might return to the scene to confuse investigators, potentially leaving false clues or engaging in behavior meant to misdirect the investigation.
- **Compulsion:** For some offenders, the act of returning to the scene may be a compulsion or an urge they cannot resist.

Understanding the behaviors and motivations of offenders is a crucial aspect of criminal profiling and investigative work. Profiling helps law enforcement gain insights into the mindset of the offender, which can assist in predicting their actions and developing strategies to apprehend them. However, it's essential to emphasize that criminal behavior is complex and can vary significantly across individuals.

Not all offenders will exhibit the same patterns or behaviors, and there are often exceptions to any given profile. It's for this reason that profiling is usually only used as a tool in conjunction with other investigative methods, such as forensic evidence, witness interviews, and behavioral analysis, to build a comprehensive picture of the case.

If the unnamed suspect is indeed the man responsible for the murder of Melissa Witt, I often wonder how often and why he chooses to return to the crime scene. I think the answer simply boils down to this: The past calls out to him with an irresistible force.

D has lived a life marked by shadows and secrets. The weight of the guilt and the haunting memory of that night hangs over him like a dark cloud. Melissa's murder was a crime of passion, of anger, of twisted desire—motivations too complex and tumultuous to untangle even for him.

In the years that followed Melissa's murder, I believe he buried the memory of that night deep within himself and moved on with his life, or so he thought. But the past has a way of clawing its way back into the present—and with the resurgence of interest in Melissa's case, the past had come for him with relentless persistence.

I believe the first time he returned to the logging road, it had been a compulsion, an impulse he couldn't resist. His subsequent return to the Ozark National Forest with Christopher was about power and control. That visit to the logging road would have been different—the forest's aura in the daylight would have been bright and peaceful, with birds singing their melodious tunes and the scent of pine filling the air.

In contrast, the night he strangled Melissa, he arrived in the forest under the cover of darkness. Everything would have looked different in the moonlight—silent, timeless, and heavy with the echoes of his crime. Those memories would be impossible to shake—even for him. And as he stood again with Christopher at the very spot where he had snuffed out Melissa's life, he felt something he hadn't expected: regret. Not the kind of regret that came from fear of consequences, but a deeper, gnawing regret for the life he had taken. And he wept, his tears mixing with the soil that once cradled Melissa's body.

He wasn't seeking forgiveness; he knows he doesn't deserve it. Instead, he was seeking something he couldn't quite define—a way to make sense of the senseless, and a way to feel powerful and in control.

I often wonder if he continues to visit that old forest logging road, not to atone for his sins or seek redemption, but to confront and embrace the darkness within himself. Maybe now, even as I write this, he is standing in the stillness of the Ozark National Forest, surrounded by the echoes of his past, letting the weight of his guilt wash over him as he immerses himself in the details of Melissa Witt's murder.

But that old logging road won't hold its secrets forever. And with the help of Jay C. Rider and Chris Boyd, I am determined to unearth them, once and for all.

Chapter 11: Violence Against Women

In the United States, violence against women is a pervasive and deeply troubling issue that affects millions of lives each year. While progress has been made in raising awareness and addressing the root causes of gender-based violence, the reality is that women continue to face alarming rates of abuse, harassment, and discrimination across the country. While men and others face abuse as well, I want to focus here specifically on violence against women.

One of the most glaring examples of violence against women in the United States is domestic violence. According to the National Coalition Against Domestic Violence (NCADV), an estimated 1 in 4 women will experience severe physical violence by an intimate partner in their lifetime. This staggering statistic highlights the pervasive nature of domestic violence and the profound impact it has on women's lives.

Domestic violence can take many forms, including physical, emotional, and psychological abuse. Women who are trapped in abusive relationships often face significant barriers to seeking help, including fear of retaliation from their abusers, financial dependence, and lack of access to resources and support services.

Domestic abuse of women is a harrowing reality that can escalate to murder, shattering lives and devastating families in its wake. One such tragic case that underscores this grim reality is the story of Lauren McCluskey, a 21-year-old student athlete at the University of Utah.

In September 2018, Lauren McCluskey was in a relationship with Melvin Shawn Rowland, a man she met on campus. Initially, their relationship appeared to be like any other, but as time went on, Lauren began to notice troubling signs of possessiveness and control from Shawn.

Lauren's friends and family became increasingly concerned about her well-being as they witnessed Shawn's escalating behavior. He would often call and text Lauren incessantly, demanding to know her whereabouts and who she was with. Despite their warnings, Lauren was reluctant to end the relationship, fearing Shawn's reaction.

As the abuse intensified, Lauren made the courageous decision to break things off with Shawn for good. However, Shawn's response was anything but accepting. Enraged by the rejection, he became increasingly volatile and began to threaten Lauren's safety.

On the evening of October 22, 2018, Lauren was returning to her dormitory after a night class when she was ambushed by Shawn in the parking lot. In a fit of rage, Shawn grabbed Lauren and forced her into a car at gunpoint. He then drove her to a remote location off campus, where he brutally strangled her to death before taking his own life.

The news of Lauren's tragic death sent shockwaves through the University of Utah community and beyond, sparking a national conversation about domestic violence and the need for greater support and resources for victims. Lauren's family and loved ones were left devastated by her senseless murder, grappling with the pain of losing a beloved daughter, sister, and friend.

Lauren McCluskey's story serves as a poignant reminder of the terrible impact of domestic abuse in dating relationships. But her story, sadly, is not unique. In 2021, Gabby Petito's tragic death captured the attention of the nation and brought renewed focus to issues of domestic violence and missing persons cases. Her story serves as a sobering reminder of the dangers faced by women in abusive relationships and the importance of taking action to protect those who are vulnerable.

Gabby, a 22-year-old aspiring travel blogger from Long Island, New York, embarked on a cross-country road trip with her fiancé, Brian Laundrie, in the summer of 2021. The couple documented their travels on social media, sharing photos and videos of their adventures as they visited national parks and scenic landmarks across the United States.

But as their journey continued, troubling signs began to emerge. Friends and family members noticed that Gabby's posts on social media became less frequent, and she seemed to grow increasingly distant and anxious in her communications with loved ones. Concerned for her well-being, Gabby's mother reported her missing to authorities in late August.

The search for Gabby intensified in the days and weeks that followed, as law enforcement agencies and volunteers combed through vast wilderness areas and remote campsites in search of any sign of her whereabouts. Meanwhile, Brian Laundrie returned to his parents' home in Florida without Gabby, raising suspicions about his involvement in her disappearance.

On September 19, 2021, human remains believed to be those of Gabby Petito were discovered in a remote area of Grand Teton National Park in Wyoming. The news sent shockwaves across the country, as millions of people had been following Gabby's story and now mourned the loss of a young woman whose life was cut tragically short. An autopsy later revealed that Gabby died from blunt-force injuries to her head and neck and manual strangulation.

In the weeks that followed, authorities launched a nationwide manhunt for Brian Laundrie, who was no longer with his parents and had not been seen since he had become the subject of intense scrutiny in connection with Gabby's death. On October 20, 2021, human remains believed to be those of Brian Laundrie were discovered in a Florida nature reserve, bringing an end to the search for him.

Gabby Petito's death sparked a much-needed national conversation about domestic violence, missing persons cases, and the need for greater support and resources for victims of abuse.

Shortly after Gabby's remains were found, I was sitting alone at the conference table in my office, immersed in a sea of reports detailing the disturbing pattern of abuse against women attributed to our unnamed suspect. The sheer volume and gravity of those allegations were overwhelming, painting a portrait of a man with a dark and violent history.

As I read through each report, my heart sank further with the realization that this suspect might indeed be the one responsible for Melissa Witt's murder. The mounting evidence, both from these reports and the revelations within Melissa's diary, pointed to a sinister and dangerous man.

"He held me at gunpoint," one woman reported.

"He stalked me by sitting outside the parking lot of my office, and then he slashed my tires," another said.

"I was punched in the face repeatedly."

"He put his hands around my neck to strangle me," another terrified woman confided in me. "I thought he was going to kill me."

His history of violence against women, coupled with his contradictory alibis, lies, and erratic behavior, leaves little room for doubt—the man whose name starts with the letter D warrants a much closer look.

Three weeks later, I would discover just how relevant and significant this line of thinking would prove to be.

After finishing a book talk in Little Rock, Arkansas, a woman, clearly in distress, approached me with trembling hands and a desperate look in her eyes. She wore dark sunglasses to conceal a black eye as well as a wig, evidently trying to hide her identity. She asked hesitantly, "LaDonna Humphrey?"

I nodded in acknowledgment, my concern growing as she continued, "I just moved out of my boyfriend's house. He's incredibly violent, LaDonna."

"Sit down," I said as I motioned to a nearby table and chairs. "Let me see if I can get you some help."

"No!" she barked. "You don't understand. I drove here to tell you…. I need you to know… I think he killed Melissa Witt."

Her outburst, "he killed Melissa Witt," was like a bombshell that exploded in the room, sending shockwaves through everyone present. The sudden revelation sent the rest of the room scurrying out the front door.

After the room cleared and we were alone, I asked her, "Who is it that you think killed Melissa?"

She hesitated for a moment, her eyes filled with a mixture of fear and sorrow, before finally revealing the haunting truth. "my ex-boyfriend," she whispered, her voice trembling. As she uttered the name of our suspect— the name that starts with the letter D—I sat down next to her.

"I think you're right," I answered gently, placing my hand on her arm. "But right now, we need to focus on you. Let's get you some help."

According to a 2007 (revised in 2009) U.S. Department of Justice, Female Victims of Violent Study, women made up 70% of victims killed by an intimate partner—a proportion that has changed very little since 1993. Additionally, the study concluded that females were killed by intimate partners at twice the rate of males.

These statistics align with the theory that our suspect, a man who had dated Melissa Witt, could be her killer. These facts underscore the importance of thoroughly examining D's history and behavior.

I am haunted by the fact that a predator was lurking within the shadows of Melissa's innocent teenage life. Someone whose sinister intentions eventually led to her murder. And now, the pursuit of justice for Melissa Witt has taken on a renewed sense of urgency. He cannot remain hidden forever, and it is my mission to ensure that the truth prevails and that justice is served not only for Melissa, but for every woman that this monster has abused.

Chapter 12: Chloroform Girl

The day was winding down when my cell phone buzzed with an incoming call. The caller ID displayed "Nixon O'Neil," a name I hadn't seen in months.

Curiosity piqued, I answered the call. "Nixon? It's been a while. How have you been?"

Nixon's voice sounded strained, and there was an urgency in his tone that immediately caught my attention. "I'm in Northwest Arkansas for business," he explained hastily. "I need to meet with you, LaDonna. It's important, and it can't wait."

His words sent a shiver down my spine. I hadn't heard from Nixon in ages, and the urgency in his request made me take pause. "Of course, Nixon," I replied, my concern growing. "I'm available. Where and when do you want to meet?"

Nixon wasted no time. "Let's meet at the Pinnacle Grill at 7:00 PM. It's a quiet place, and we can talk there. I'll explain everything then."

As I agreed to the meeting, Nixon's voice dropped to a hushed tone. "LaDonna, I've been receiving strange text messages lately. I think he knows you are on to him. I fear for your safety. This might be a threat."

The mention of the unnamed suspect sent a chill down my spine. The case had become increasingly complex, and the suspect was aware of my suspicions. I thanked Nixon for the warning and assured him that I would be cautious.

As the evening approached, I drove to the restaurant, my thoughts consumed by the unfolding mystery. The Pinnacle Grill was nestled in a quiet corner of Northwest Arkansas, its cozy atmosphere providing a semblance of solace amidst the uncertainty that lay ahead.

Nixon O'Neil was already seated at a corner table, his face etched with concern. As I approached, he greeted me with a solemn nod, and we exchanged a brief, anxious glance before settling into our chairs.

Nixon wasted no time, taking out his phone and showing me the series of text messages he had received. The messages were eerie, containing lyrics from the song "Chloroform Girl" by Polkadot Cadaver. The connection between the lyrics and the chilling atmosphere surrounding Melissa Witt's murder was impossible to ignore.

His voice trembled with fear as he spoke. "LaDonna, I'm convinced these texts are from my old roommate. It's not a coincidence. He knows that you suspect him in Melissa's murder, and I think he's sending these texts as a threat."

As I read through the lyrics of "Chloroform Girl," a sense of fear and foreboding settled over me. The words seemed like a dark and ominous message. It was undeniable. This was more than just a coincidence.

"Chloroform girl, how have you been? Don't let me catch you sleeping again. You're only alive because I like you. It's been three years since you've seen the sunlight, but I know you're having fun—bound, gagged and chained up in my basement."

The choice of those specific lyrics, with their ominous undertones, felt deliberate and calculated. It was as if the sender of those texts wanted to instill fear and unease, to make it clear that they were watching, waiting, and capable of darker deeds. This was not a mere prank or random occurrence. It felt like a direct threat, a message meant to instill fear and convey a sense of impending doom. I couldn't deny the unsettling feeling that washed over me. The danger was real, and the web of deception and darkness surrounding the case was closing in.

As I glanced up from the phone, I met Nixon's eyes, and we shared a silent understanding of the gravity of the situation. The pursuit of justice for Melissa Witt had taken a dangerous turn, and the stakes were higher than ever before.

"I think he's a sociopath," Nixon blurted out before leaning in closer, his voice hushed as he shared this chilling insight. "He meets the definition of a sociopath—charming, intelligent, superficial, outwardly friendly, and extremely dangerous," he began, his words carrying the weight of grim experience with the old roommate he now feared.

He continued, "Sociopathic, psychopathic, and antisocial personalities are all closely related and have been defined as personality types exhibiting a profound and usually untreatable form of abnormal behavior." Nixon's eyes bore the weight of the knowledge he was imparting, acquired through years of friendship with his old roommate.

"Many mass murderers, rapists, and a large percentage of habitual criminals exhibit the lack of guilt and the need for instant gratification characteristic of this behavior type," he added.

Nixon's revelation about sociopathic behavior was profound. As I reflected on his words, a gnawing sense of unease settled in the pit of my stomach. The more I delved into the suspect's past and actions, the more Nixon's assessment seemed alarmingly accurate.

Nixon's words painted a picture of the sociopathic personality, one devoid of empathy and driven by selfish desires. His experience had shown him that these individuals often operated under the radar, using their charming facade to manipulate and deceive those around them.

The room seemed to grow colder as the tale unfolded. "He's done horrible things," Nixon admitted, "and has shown no remorse for any of it." His words left a chilling echo in the room. It became clear that understanding the mind of the suspect would be a crucial element in unraveling the dark secrets surrounding the Witt case.

Just as we exited the Pinnacle Grill to head to our cars, Nixon said, "LaDonna, there's something else you need to know," his tone gravely serious. "He's also obsessed with the murder of Nona Dirksmeyer."

The mention of another murder case, one that had haunted the River Valley community for years, caught me off guard. Nona Dirksmeyer, a 19-year-old Arkansas Tech University student and Miss Arkansas contestant was found murdered on December 15, 2005 in her apartment. Dirksmeyer was brutally stabbed and beaten to death with the base of her own floor lamp. The case remains unsolved.

"He's researched the case, collected news articles, and even reached out to law enforcement agencies about it. It's become an all-consuming obsession for him," Nixon explained.

"That is bizarre," I muttered to myself as I settled into my car. The revelations from Nixon about his old roommate's obsessions with both Melissa Witt's murder and Nona Dirksmeyer's unsolved case had left my mind racing with questions.

I started the engine and began to drive, my thoughts consumed by D and his actions. What else had he done? What secrets were still hidden beneath the surface? The more I delved into the investigation, the more it felt like an invisible thread was binding me to the unnamed suspect. Each revelation, each piece of evidence, seemed to draw me closer to the enigmatic figure at the center of the mystery.

And as the web of connections grew more complex with each passing day, I couldn't shake the feeling that I was on the verge of uncovering something significant.

Chapter 13: Nona Dirksmeyer

On December 15, 2005, in the heart of Russellville, Arkansas, Nona Dirksmeyer, a 19-year-old beauty queen and Arkansas Tech University student, became the central figure in a tragic story that remains unresolved. The teenager's apartment transformed into the setting of a brutal crime that shocked the community and baffled investigators.

Nona Dirksmeyer, with her dynamic personality and high aspirations, had become an integral part of Russellville's community. Her active participation in beauty pageants and academic life at Arkansas Tech University had positioned her as a young woman standing on the threshold of a bright future, fully engaged in the life of her town and university.

However, Nona Dirksmeyer's once hopeful future was tragically cut short when her boyfriend, Kevin Jones, stumbled upon her lifeless nude body. The crime scene painted a chilling picture of violence: Nona had been punched in the face with such force that it caused bruising on her brain. The presence of shallow stab wounds across her neck and shoulders indicated a relentless attack by someone consumed with rage. But the horror doesn't stop there. Nona was also strangled. And like Melissa, she was choked so violently that the hyoid bone in her neck was broken.

There was no evidence of forced entry, and this led investigators to believe that Nona's killer was potentially someone she knew quite well. Initial suspicion fell upon her boyfriend, Kevin, whose fingerprints were found on the alleged murder weapon—a lampstand. He was eventually charged with her murder. However, the absence of forced entry, along with the presence of a condom wrapper not linked to Kevin, and a botched police investigation led to his acquittal, leaving the community with more questions than answers.

As the town of Russellville continued to grapple with the shock of Nona's murder, a new suspect emerged from the shadows: Gary Dunn, a neighbor with a checkered past. Dunn's DNA, discovered on the condom wrapper at the crime scene, painted him as a plausible perpetrator. The trials that followed were a testament to the complexities of the legal system—two separate juries were unable to reach a unanimous verdict.

In the wake of the trials, the community was left divided. The media frenzy that enveloped the case did little to aid in the search for the truth. Instead Nona's murder was sensationalized—every detail, every lead, and every setback, turned the tragedy into a spectacle.

Nona's murder captured the attention of more than just the media. Among those drawn to the details of the case was someone who blended into the background yet harbored an unsettling interest in the darker aspects of human nature. This person, our unnamed suspect in the Witt murder, found himself particularly engrossed in the intricacies of the Dirksmeyer case.

And according to Nixon O'Neil, the suspect's old roommate, his fascination wasn't merely that of a casual observer; it was an obsession that consumed his thoughts. He meticulously followed every update, collected newspaper clippings, and spent countless hours online, diving into forums and discussion boards where theories and accusations ran rampant. His interest was not driven by a desire for justice or a quest for truth but by a morbid curiosity and a need to understand the mind of the perpetrator.

As the investigation into Nona's untimely death unfolded, revealing a tangled web of relationships and motives, I have to wonder if our unnamed suspect found parallels between himself and the individuals at the center of the case. He was particularly drawn to the scrutiny placed on the suspects, analyzing their behaviors, their interactions with law enforcement, and the public's perception of their guilt or innocence. It was as if he was studying, learning, and assessing how well they navigated the suspicion that enveloped them.

After Nixon tipped me off about the suspect's activities on online forums discussing Nona's case, I dove headfirst into the digital depths where these conversations thrived. The online world, with its labyrinth of discussion boards, blogs, and comment sections, became my new investigative battleground.

Armed with determination and a keen eye for detail, I meticulously sifted through countless posts, comments, and threads. The anonymity of the internet often emboldens individuals to reveal more about themselves than they might in person, and I was counting on this very thing to work in my favor. Instead, I discovered something unexpected. Our suspect was inside those forums under his real name, and he was openly discussing the intricacies of Nona's murder with an unsettling level of engagement. This revelation was shocking.

His posts, which dissected various aspects of the investigation and trial, revealed a keen observer who had taken the time to study the case in minute detail. His posts were analytical, and often speculative, weaving complex theories that diverted attention away from the main suspects. It was clear from his writing that he had invested a significant amount of time in following the case, absorbing every detail and every development with an intensity that bordered on obsession. This wasn't merely a pastime for him; it was a morbid fascination that he seemed unable to shake off. This involvement in online discussions about the case suggested that the suspect saw Nona's tragic story not just as a crime to be analyzed but a learning opportunity.

The information I gathered from the forums became a valuable asset in my ongoing investigation into Melissa Witt's murder. It provided insight into the suspect's mind, his methods, and perhaps most importantly, his arrogance. He believed himself to be untouchable, a master manipulator hidden behind the veil of the internet. But with each post, he unwittingly provided us with the means to unravel his web of deceit, bringing us one step closer to the truth.

As I sifted through his online activity, I found myself grappling with a crucial question: Why was he so fixated on this particular case? The intensity of his interest seemed to go beyond mere curiosity or the allure of a high-profile crime story. It was as if he was drawing something more personal, more profound from the information.

Several possibilities began to emerge as I pondered this question. Was there a psychological thrill in immersing himself in the details of another crime, especially one that had captured so much public attention? The Dirksmeyer case, with its twists, turns, and the emotional rollercoaster it presented, could offer a dark form of vicarious excitement for someone inclined toward such interests.

Another angle to consider was the sense of power and control. By engaging deeply with the case, offering theories, and steering conversations, our suspect might have experienced a feeling of influence over how the case was perceived by others. This control, even if only exercised in the virtual realm of online forums, could satisfy a deep-seated need to dominate and manipulate narratives, reflecting a dangerous aspect of his personality.

Moreover, was there an element of identification or empathy with the accused or the victim in the Dirksmeyer case? Sometimes, individuals with certain psychological profiles might see aspects of themselves in the participants of such dramas, whether it be the victim's vulnerability or the accused's situation of being under suspicion. This identification could drive an obsession, as the suspect seeks to understand, justify, or relive aspects of the case that resonate with his own experiences or fantasies.

Our suspect's engagement with the Dirksmeyer case might also serve as a form of rehearsal or research. By analyzing the investigation's progress, the public's reaction, and the judicial outcomes, he could be gathering information for his own nefarious purposes. Understanding how certain actions lead to certain results, what mistakes were made, and how suspects were either convicted or acquitted could provide valuable lessons for someone contemplating similar crimes. In addition, the trials, with their public scrutiny and legal maneuvers, provided him with a real-time case study on how criminal investigations unfold, how evidence is presented and challenged, and how public opinion can be swayed by media coverage.

Or was it possible that there was a more direct connection between our suspect and the Dirksmeyer case? While this seemed like a less likely scenario given the available information, it is not entirely out of the realm of possibility. Our suspect's deep involvement might hint at personal ties to the case or the people involved, whether through direct acquaintance, geographical proximity, or a more obscure link that has yet to be uncovered.

As I continued my investigation, these questions remained at the forefront of my mind. Understanding the root of D's obsession with the Dirksmeyer case could be key to unraveling his psyche and, ultimately, his involvement in the crimes he is suspected of committing. It was a complex puzzle, but one that needs to be solved to prevent further harm and bring justice to those affected.

Chapter 14: Fraternity Brothers

Almost thirty years had passed since Mark and Mike had been fraternity brothers. The memories of their college days were a mix of camaraderie and dread, as they had witnessed the dark side of one of their frat brothers—our unnamed suspect. A cloud of unease had hung over them for decades, and now, after all these years, they couldn't bear the weight of their silence any longer.

Late one evening, as Mark and Mike sat in their respective homes, they decided to take action. They had heard about my work on the Witt case and my pursuit for justice for Melissa, so they reached out to me via email:

"Mrs. Humphrey, we (myself and a friend) have some information about one of our fraternity brothers that may be of interest to you. We are aware that he had some sort of relationship with Melissa Witt. We also know how violent and abusive he was toward women back then. We would like to meet with you."

I responded immediately and arranged to meet both men at a quiet, discreet coffee shop not far from their hometown. As we gathered around the table, our

Styrofoam cups in hand, the two men began to share the haunting memories of their time in the fraternity house.

"We've kept this secret for two decades," Mike admitted, his voice quivering with emotion. "But it's time the truth came out."

The fraternity brothers went on to recount the chilling incidents they had witnessed from our suspect during their college days. His violent temper, his abusive behavior toward women, and the fear he instilled in everyone around him were laid bare.

"We were young and scared back then," Mark confessed. "But we can't let his actions go unpunished any longer."

Mike's confession was equally troubling. "I've witnessed him slapping women," he said with a heavy sigh. "And I've heard him brag numerous times about forcing himself on women who have passed out drunk." His words painted a chilling picture of our suspect's behavior and attitudes toward women.

My heart sank as I listened to these horrifying accounts. It was clear that our unnamed suspect had a history of violence and aggression toward women, a pattern of behavior that is deeply unsettling. These revelations only added to the mounting evidence against him.

After the conversation ended, I assured Mark and Mike that I would investigate their claims rigorously. The pursuit of justice for Melissa Witt was now fueled not only by the memories of two fraternity brothers but also by their determination to ensure that the darkness they had witnessed all those years ago was finally exposed.

As I exited the coffee shop after our meeting, I realized I needed to reach out to Nixon to gather more information that could potentially shed light on this case.

I dialed his number, my heart racing with anticipation, and listened to the ringing on the other end. Each ring seemed to stretch on endlessly until finally, a voice answered. It was Nixon O'Neil, our suspect's old roommate—a potential key witness in this complex puzzle.

I introduced myself and explained the reason for my call, emphasizing the importance of his recollection of events from our unnamed suspect's college days. During our conversation, I asked Nixon to share more details about what our suspect told him regarding the women he assaulted in college. His voice held a mixture of surprise and concern as he listened to and answered my questions.

After our call disconnected, I knew the next step was to confront the unnamed suspect directly. I picked up my phone and dialed his number.

The phone rang, and my mind raced as I rehearsed the questions I needed to ask. His voice on the other end was calm and collected, but I could sense a subtle tension beneath the surface as I inquired, "Can you tell me about your college days? Tell me about some of the girls you dated."

His response was measured, his words chosen carefully, "Why do you want to know that?" he finally responded.

"Were you ever violent with anyone you dated?" I asked.

He paused. "Who knows. Who cares? I don't remember that far back," he replied.

"You don't know or care if you were violent with women you dated?" I asked tauntingly. "Interesting."

"I've done a lot of drugs, drank a lot of booze since then," he offered. "But I know I wasn't violent with Melissa if that's the real question you are getting at."

"Are you *certain*?" I asked

"Positive," he responded.

As the conversation continued, I pressed for more details, hoping to uncover any information that might lead us closer to the truth.

Suddenly, and with an angry tone, he blurted out, "She wanted to marry me."

"She barely knew you," I quickly retorted.

"I loved her," he responded. "I loved her so much."

"Oh yeah?" I said tauntingly. "Is that so?"

There was an uncomfortable silence between us as I thought back to the diary entries Melissa had written about him: "I'm not really interested in him."

"I've totally forgotten about him now," she wrote.

"I'm not calling him again."

I decided to shatter the quiet anticipation that was suffocating both of us. My voice, steady but resolute, echoed through the phone. "I have read her diary," I confessed. "I *know* what she thought about you."

The words hung in the air, and, for a brief moment, there was nothing but the sound of his slow, shallow breathing. Then, on the other end of the line, there was a sharp intake of breath, and his voice crackled with anger and anxiety. "What are you talking about?" he demanded, his tone defensive.

The fear and unease in his response only fueled my determination to get to the truth. "Melissa's diary," I continued. "It paints a different picture of you…"

Before I could continue, the line went dead.

Chapter 15: Masks

As my husband Danny stood amidst the echoing cheers and the rhythmic bounce of the basketball at our youngest son's tournament, his world came to a standstill. The glaring lights of the gymnasium seemed to dim as he read the message again, hoping he had misunderstood. The words on the screen were unyielding in their intent: "I'm sorry for what I just did to your family. Goodbye." His mind raced, trying to comprehend who would send such a threat and why.

With trembling hands, he dialed my number, his gaze fixed on the court where our son, Jaxon, oblivious to the unfolding drama, played with his team. Each ring of the call felt like an eternity, amplifying his fear. The bustling sounds of the game around him turned into a distant murmur as his focus narrowed to the phone in his hand. When I didn't answer his call, a sense of dread enveloped him, thick and suffocating.

He attempted to steady his breathing, to quell the rising panic. The safety of his family was paramount, and he knew he needed to act swiftly. He signaled to Jaxon, indicating an urgent need to leave. The confusion on our son's face mirrored the turmoil within Danny, but there was no time for explanations.

As they hurried to the car, Danny's mind was a whirlwind of worst-case scenarios. The drive home was a blur, each turn and stop light punctuating his growing apprehension.

When Danny arrived home, the sight that greeted him was one of chaos and confusion. Police cars with their lights painting the night in shades of blue and red illuminated the driveway. As he jumped out of his truck, our eyes met in a silent exchange of a myriad of emotions that ranged from fear, determination, and unspoken resolve.

"I think this is related to the Witt case," I blurted out.

"What happened?" Danny asked, his voice filled with panic.

I explained how a black truck had pulled up in front of our house and blared its horn before driving away quickly. And by the time the truck made a second and then a third ominous pass, the situation had escalated from curious to alarming.

"The truck came back for a fourth time, blared their horn, and parked," I explained. "Two figures emerged, their identities obscured by Halloween masks that transformed their appearance into something grotesque and unrecognizable."

As I recounted the harrowing moments that unfolded, Danny's expression morphed into one of grave concern.

"Seconds later, the men were banging on our side door with enough force that our house shook," I explained. "My instincts kicked in and I ordered the kids upstairs— and then I grabbed the shotgun." When I mentioned grabbing the shotgun, my husband's seriousness deepened, a mixture of admiration and concern etched on his face.

"And then," I said shakily, "they suddenly stopped— and just as swiftly and mysteriously as they arrived, the masked men vanished into the night." As I shared our horrifying experience, I knew in my heart that this was no random act of vandalism or misguided prank. It was a clear and targeted attempt to intimidate.

After absorbing the gravity of this, Danny reached for his cell phone. He scrolled through his messages, finding the ominous text that had sent him rushing home. As he handed me the phone, he watched as my eyes scanned the message, my expression shifting from concern to dawning realization.

The timing of the text message, sent mere seconds before the arrival of the menacing truck and its honking horn, was too precise to be coincidental. The synchronization of the events painted a clear picture of a premeditated campaign of fear. As I read the words on Danny's phone, the chilling threat echoed in my mind, casting the evening's events in a new light.

As I lifted my gaze from the glowing screen of Danny's phone, a sudden realization crystallized in my mind, bringing with it a chilling clarity. "One of the men was wearing a President Nixon mask," I stated, my voice steady despite the turmoil swirling within my heart.

The mention of the Nixon mask cast a shadow of deeper significance over the events. My mind raced as I drew a connection to Nixon O'Neil, a recent pivotal figure in the Witt case. The coincidence, if it was one, was too stark to ignore. The symbolic choice of a Nixon mask could not be overlooked, its implications far-reaching. Was it a deliberate message, a taunt from those who wished to remain hidden in the shadows? Or was it merely a random selection by the masked intruders, devoid of any deeper meaning?

The possibility that the mask was a direct reference to Nixon O'Neil, and by extension, to the unnamed suspect in my investigation, sent a ripple of fear through my body. The thought that my work had drawn the attention of those willing to go to such lengths to intimidate me was both alarming and a testament to the significance of the secrets I was fighting to uncover.

My entire family, once a haven of normalcy and routine, had found themselves thrust into a narrative they had never anticipated—one where the lines between my work and their personal lives blurred dangerously. The incident with the truck and the masked figures was not just an attack on our home but an assault on our sense of security.

Remarkably, even in the face of this orchestrated terror, the resolve within my family only solidified. Together, we recognized the necessity of standing united, of bolstering our defenses, both physical and emotional, against the threats that loomed large at our doorstep. This episode, harrowing as it was, served to strengthen our bond, and our courage.

With the weight of the night's events bearing down on me, I knew it was time to seek counsel and support from someone I trusted implicitly: Jay C. Rider. His friendship, expertise, and insight had been invaluable to me in the past, and now, more than ever, I needed his guidance.

I picked up the phone and dialed Rider's number. When he answered, his voice was a beacon of calm in the storm that had engulfed my life. "Rider, something happened tonight," I began, my voice steady but laced with an undercurrent of tension. I proceeded to recount my frightening experience, from the ominous arrival of the truck and its blaring horn to the menacing figures in masks, one hauntingly donning the visage of President Nixon.

As I spoke, I could almost sense Rider's mind working, piecing together the implications of my story, the potential connections to the Witt case, and the unnerving symbolism of the Nixon mask. His responses were measured, a mix of concern for my safety and a professional curiosity about the possible motives behind the intimidation.

Rider's advice was pragmatic, emphasizing the importance of safety and caution. He suggested documenting every detail of the incident, no matter how insignificant it might seem, and enhancing security measures around my home. But more than that, Rider offered his support, assuring me that I was not alone in this fight. "We need to tread carefully," he advised, "but we have to press on."

I felt a wave of relief wash over me as I spoke with Rider. His presence, even over the phone, was a grounding force, reminding me of the strength found in solidarity. The conversation with him was not just a strategic discussion; it was a reaffirmation of our shared commitment to seeking the truth, no matter the obstacles thrown in our path.

As our call ended, I felt a renewed sense of purpose. The events of the night had been a reminder of the risks involved in my investigative work, but the support of allies like Jay C. Rider bolstered my resolve. Together, we would continue to navigate the unknown waters of this investigation, confronting the shadows with the light of our unwavering quest for justice for Melissa Witt.

Chapter 16: The Fetishers

Despite the unsettling encounter with the masked men at my doorstep, my determination to uncover the truth in the Witt case did not waver. Instead, the incident served to reinforce my commitment, propelling me further into my investigative pursuits—including what had become my new and equally crucial mission: to dismantle and expose the sinister underbelly of the death fetish community.

I stumbled upon death fetish after a lead in the Melissa Witt investigation steered me toward this dark and hidden segment of society that serves as a breeding ground for the macabre and the unlawful. As part of the Witt investigation, and with the support of law enforcement, I infiltrated this online community with the intention of unraveling its secrets. I aimed to disrupt its operations, protect potential victims, and challenge the very foundations that allowed such a community to flourish unchecked, all while gathering information for the Witt case. This dual focus on solving a cold case and combating a present-day menace represented a broadening of my fight against the darkest aspects of human behavior, making my investigative work not just a pursuit of truth, but a crusade for the safety and dignity of those most vulnerable.

The thought that someone from Melissa's own circle, a name penned in the pages of her diary, might harbor such dark obsessions began to take root. The possibility that this individual's fascination with violent and death fetish pornography could be the missing link in the puzzle was a disturbing revelation. This angle suggested a deeply personal connection to Melissa, one that intertwined her tragic fate with the sinister undercurrents of a hidden community. It was a lead that, although speculative, opened new avenues that might possibly uncover the private obsessions of those closest to Melissa. A year after my online undercover investigation began, I ventured even further into the abyss of these hidden horrors by launching the *Deep Dark Secrets* podcast. This new platform allowed me to delve deeper into these online communities while engaging with a broader audience, sharing insights, gathering tips, and rallying support against the grotesque exploitation found within the death fetish online forums.

However, as you can imagine, this work, while rewarding, has not been without its perils. The deeper I probe, the more resistance I encounter, manifesting in threats and intimidation, similar to the sinister visit from the masked intruders. And even though shining a light on this dark community has placed me in the crosshairs of those who thrive in the shadows, I wholeheartedly believe the importance of the mission outweighs the personal risks.

This was especially true one afternoon as I navigated the dark corridors of this horrible online world and stumbled upon a username that made my heart skip a beat: StrangledMW. The sinister undertone of this moniker was unmistakable, suggesting a disturbing link or, perhaps, a deliberate taunt aimed at the core of my ongoing investigation into Melissa Witt's murder. The posts associated with this account were deeply unsettling, weaving a narrative that felt both personal and menacing. The brazen admissions, such as "I strangled her slowly," coupled with morbid proclamations like "I love strangled women in the forest," painted a picture of someone not just obsessed with their twisted fantasies but possibly re-enacting them in the most horrific ways.

These forum posts seemed to be more than just the ramblings of a disturbed individual; they appeared to be calculated, designed to provoke a reaction, or, worse, lure me deeper into a dangerous interaction. The specificity of the comments, the deliberate references to strangulation, and the choice of setting in a forest—a detail eerily reminiscent of Melissa's case made me take pause. Concerned, I dug deeper, only to discover something truly frightening: Many of StrangledMW's posts dated back almost a decade *before* my investigation into the Witt case began.

As I read through the labyrinth of posts, I was shocked to discover StrangledMW disclosed his real name, one that intriguingly began with the letter D—the same as the unnamed suspect in the Witt investigation. As I sat transfixed by the glow of the computer screen, the revelation that this could be a direct connection to the Witt case was far too significant to dismiss.

I reached for my phone, my fingers moving with purpose as I composed a message to Nixon O'Neil. The question was direct, cutting through any potential for ambiguity: "Was your old roommate into violent porn?" The reply came swiftly, chilling in its brevity and implication: "Yes. He's addicted to that shit."

The response triggered a cascade of thoughts, leading me back to the unsettling song lyrics of "Chloroform Girl" that the unnamed suspect had once sent to Nixon. The song resonated with dark, haunting undertones. Its lyrics painted a grim portrait of a toxic and abusive relationship, delving into themes of control, obsession, and a perverse delight in the suffering of another. The disturbing nature of the song, coupled with the new information provided by Nixon, seemed to weave together a sinister tapestry, hinting at the depths of the suspect's depravity and potentially offering a new angle from which to approach the investigation.

The initial lead that guided us toward the dark waters of the death fetish community came from a harrowing account by a woman who recounted her experience in creating a film with a death fetish producer—a video that centered around her simulated death by strangulation while wearing a Mickey Mouse watch. The detail about the Mickey Mouse watch struck a haunting chord, given its eerie connection to the Melissa Witt case. This link, seemingly trivial yet oddly specific, hinted at a deeper, more sinister undercurrent that could potentially tie the fetish community to the case in ways previously unimagined.

While this lead piqued our interest and pulled us in deeper, it unfortunately did not culminate in the identification of Melissa Witt's killer. Hitting a dead end was frustrating, yet it sparked a pivotal reconsideration of our approach. Perhaps our angle had been too narrow, our focus misplaced.

Now, in my pursuit to uncover the truth, I decided to directly engage with StrangledMW. Crafting my message with a blend of caution and determination, I introduced myself, "This is LaDonna Humphrey." Then I highlighted my investigative journey through the death fetish community that led me to his intriguing posts. "I have been reading through your messages in this forum and I came across a post where you provided your name," I stated, setting the stage for my inquiry. Then, cutting to the core of my suspicions, I posed a critical question, "Did you know Melissa Witt?"

Three days later, I received a terse and hostile response: "You stupid bitch, mind your own business." His vulgarity and aggression fueled my defiant retort: "I think I know who this is. Why don't you just text me? You already have my phone number." It was a bold move, one I hoped would spark a personal confrontation.

However, my attempt at direct engagement was swiftly met with retribution. Within moments of sending my reply, I found myself expelled from the dark enclave of the forum, my screen name rendered useless and banned from re-entry. This sudden exile from the forum, while frustrating, did not deter me. I created a new account, and as soon as I regained access, I was shocked to discover that StrangledMW had vanished without a trace. The only remnants of his presence were the screenshots I had meticulously recorded earlier, tangible evidence of the conversations and posts that once existed. This sudden disappearance raised more questions than answers. Who was StrangledMW? And was he somehow connected to the Witt case?

At the exact same time I was grappling with the sudden disappearance of StrangledMW from the forum, my husband, Danny, received an email that sent chills down my spine. The sender, using the creepy moniker "Shock Gore Whore," sent a message laced with ominous undertones:

"Danny Humphrey, Your wife is a podcaster, no? She has only scratched the surface of death fetish. We want to show her the murky depths. Soon.—Geremy Ghoul"

The chilling words echoed in my mind, a warning that my investigative endeavors into the death fetish community had not gone unnoticed. The reference to "murky depths" suggested there were layers of depravity I had yet to uncover, and the sign-off, "Geremy Ghoul," added a personal and sinister touch to the message. This alarming email was a clear indication that the stakes of my investigation were escalating, pulling me deeper into a world I was only beginning to understand.

In response to the unsettling email from "Shock Gore Whore," I took immediate action by reaching out to the owner of the death fetish forum. My email was straightforward, inquiring about the real identity of StrangledMW, their knowledge of the Melissa Witt case, and any information on "Shock Gore Whore" or "Geremy Ghoul." The forum owner's reply was swift, emphasizing the forum's policy against discussing or glorifying real-life crimes, and assuring me he ran a "clean" and "normal" death fetish community.

However, it was the revelation about "Geremy Ghoul" that caught me off guard. The forum owner next disclosed that although their interactions with this individual, also known as "Shock Gore Whore," had been sporadic over the years, one crucial piece of information had emerged: Geremy Ghoul reported he lived in Greenwood, Arkansas. This detail, seemingly small, sent waves of implication. Greenwood, a town not far from the epicenter of Melissa Witt's case, suddenly became an ironic new point of interest.

My own history with Greenwood traced back to the late '80s, a time of new beginnings as I transitioned from a small town in Oklahoma to this seemingly unassuming community in Arkansas. It was during this transformative period in Greenwood that I forged bonds with individuals who would, in a twist of fate, link me to Melissa Witt in ways I could never have anticipated.

These friendships, nurtured in the camaraderie of youth and shared experiences, unknowingly acted as a bridge to Melissa. The very people I had grown close to during my year in Greenwood were the same people who were instrumental in introducing Melissa to the man who would become the prime suspect in the dark cloud hanging over her story. This chilling realization was a bitter pill to swallow, complicating my involvement in the case.

The intricate web of connections, once a mere backdrop to my investigative efforts, now stood at the forefront of my consciousness. The realization that my own life was intertwined with both the victim and the suspected perpetrator brought a profound sense of gravity to my pursuit of justice. My ties to the Witt case, always complex, now bore the weight of personal history and a fateful intertwining of paths that had led me here, compelling me to confront the haunting possibility that fate had entangled me in this story from the very beginning.

Chapter 17: The Billboards

In December of 2021, to recognize the 27th anniversary of Melissa Witt's disappearance, my team organized a press conference outside the Central Mall food court in Fort Smith. The decision to hold the press conference at this location was a deliberate and symbolic gesture, chosen for its deep connection to the last moments of normalcy in Melissa Witt's life before her disappearance. On December 1, 1994, Melissa had casually dined at the mall food court with a friend, a seemingly mundane act that preceded the tragic events that unfolded that day. By choosing this site for the press conference, my team and I aimed to not only honor Melissa's memory but also to reignite public interest and awareness in her case. We hoped to unearth new leads or information that could finally lead to justice for Melissa and closure for all who knew and loved her.

The event brought together members of the community, law enforcement, and the original detectives, Jay C. Rider and Chris Boyd, who have remained dedicated to solving this case. Their presence served as a powerful reminder of the ongoing commitment to seeking justice for Melissa.

"We are here today to remind the community that we have not forgotten and we remain steadfast in our efforts to find justice for Melissa," Rider announced at the opening of the press conference. His statement echoed the sentiment of resilience and determination that has long characterized his search for answers in this case.

During the conference, we unveiled our billboard campaign that aimed to reignite public interest and gather new leads. The bold billboards, strategically placed to capture public attention, showcased a poignant photo of Melissa Witt, her eyes looking out at passersby, invoking a silent plea for justice. Emblazoned alongside her image were the haunting words: "Who Killed Melissa Witt? Someone knows." This direct appeal to the community aimed to stir the conscience of those who might hold crucial information, however small or seemingly insignificant.

Beneath the compelling question, the billboard provided important contact information for those willing to come forward: our dedicated website, whokilledmissywitt.com, and our toll-free tipline, 800-440-1922. These resources were not just lines of communication; they represented a lifeline to potentially solving a case that had lingered in the shadows for far too long.

The inclusion of these details on the billboard was designed to make it as easy as possible for individuals to share information. It was a public declaration that the pursuit of justice for Melissa Witt was ongoing and that the community could play a pivotal role in uncovering the truth. The billboard campaign was a call to action, an invitation to break the silence and bring closure to a case that has haunted the community for decades.

The response to the billboards was immediately overwhelming and beyond anything we could ever have anticipated. The sheer volume of responses required meticulous attention, as every message held the possibility of a breakthrough in the case. Each day, I found myself immersed in a sea of calls and emails. Hours were spent documenting each piece of information, no matter how small or seemingly insignificant, for law enforcement to investigate further.

A week after we launched the billboards, I received an unexpected text from Nixon O'Neil. "I heard from my old roommate today. I think the billboards are making him nervous," his message read, a statement that immediately caught my attention. The mention of his old roommate, especially in this context, was a significant development. "He's pumping me for information. He knows you suspect him," Nixon continued, revealing a layer of paranoia and concern that seemed to have been triggered by the public campaign.

The idea that Nixon's old roommate, a figure already shrouded in suspicion, was now actively seeking information and expressing nervousness about being a potential suspect, offered a new avenue of inquiry. It underscored the importance of our efforts to keep the case in the public eye and seemed to be hitting the mark: drawing out those who had remained hidden in the shadows for too long.

Seconds later, my phone alerted me to yet another message from Nixon. This time, he relayed something even more interesting. D had asked Nixon: "I heard a rumor that there is someone squarely in LaDonna's sights. She says she believes the killer is alive and that law enforcement is closer than ever to catching him. Is she talking about me, Nixon?"

The fact that Nixon's old roommate, already rattled by the billboards and my inquiries, was directly questioning his status as a suspect, revealed the mounting pressure and fear he was feeling.

The conversation relayed by Nixon painted a vivid picture of his old roommate's escalating tension and paranoia. His direct inquiry about being a suspect, following the unease stirred by the billboard campaign and all of his probing questions, suggests a deep-seated concern. This heightened state of distress, particularly in response to the increased scrutiny and the notion that law enforcement might be closing in, naturally raised questions about the underlying reasons for such fear. Was this reaction simply the result of being under a perceived microscope, or did it indicate something more, perhaps a guilty conscience? The fine line between innocent anxiety and guilt-induced fear in Nixon's old roommate's behavior was a puzzle casting a shadow of suspense over everyone involved in the investigation. This critical distinction remained shrouded in mystery, with the truth obscured by layers of complexity and conjecture.

As the investigation pressed forward, it became clear that unraveling this mystery would require a delicate balance of patience and dogged determination. Each new piece of information, each subtle clue, and every nuanced reaction could potentially lead us closer to understanding the true motivations behind his behavior. In the intricate dance of justice, where every detail held potential significance, the journey toward uncovering the truth promised to be as challenging as it was necessary. Every day, however, we continue to inch closer to the heart of the matter and to the resolution that has been just out of reach for almost thirty years.

Chapter 18: Carla Walker

The impact of the billboards on reigniting public interest in the Witt case was undeniable. One afternoon, I received an email in response to the billboard campaign that really caught my attention. The author of the email wrote about a young woman named Carla Walker, who, like Melissa, was abducted from a bowling alley parking lot and later found strangled to death.

The email provided a compelling narrative about Carla Walker's murder in Texas during the '70s, emphasizing a remarkable turn in the investigation that led to its resolution many years later. The breakthrough came through the innovative application of genealogy DNA testing, a technique that has revolutionized the approach to solving cold cases. This method, by tracing familial DNA lines, helped authorities to finally identify and apprehend the perpetrator, bringing long-awaited closure to a case that had lingered in uncertainty for decades.

As I delved into Carla's case, I came across a news story entitled "Was She His Only Victim?" This resonated with me, because I know that perpetrators often have a hidden trail of untold stories. Intrigued, I dove deeper into Carla Walker's case.

The tragic details surrounding Carla Walker's abduction and murder were heartbreaking. After a Valentine's Day dance, Carla and her boyfriend, Rodney McCoy, continued the evening's celebrations with friends. In a split-second decision, they decided to stop at a local bowling alley to use the restroom. They had no idea this would set the stage for a nightmarish turn of events.

What happened next was horrific. Walker and McCoy were blindsided by an armed gunman. The attack was swift and brutal. According to McCoy, the car door suddenly swung open and the two were assaulted by an unknown white male, who was approximately 5 foot 10 inches tall. During the brutal attack, the magazine from the man's gun fell to the ground as he violently pistol-whipped McCoy, eventually rendering him unconscious. His last memory of the incident was of Carla being forcibly removed from the car by the unknown male as she screamed for help. Once McCoy regained consciousness, he immediately searched for his girlfriend. When he realized she could not be found, he drove to the Walkers' house to inform her parents of the frightening series of events.

The family notified the police who began an immediate search of the area where Walker had been abducted. Her purse and the gun magazine were the only items recovered in the parking lot. Sadly, on February 20, 1974, Walker's body was found in a culvert in Lake Benbrook. The autopsy revealed that she had been alive for two days following her abduction. The report also revealed that she had been beaten, tortured, raped, and strangled to death. And, according to the toxicology report, she had also been injected with morphine.

The police were able to obtain samples of bodily fluids from the crime scene. Walker's dress and other clothing were also preserved. Unfortunately, technology to test such samples to identify the killer did not exist in the 1970s, so the Walker case sat cold for almost four decades. Finally, on September 21, 2020, investigators arrested 77-year-old Glen McCurley, a retired truck driver, maintenance worker, and ex-convict, after his DNA matched the DNA found on Carla Walker's clothes all those years ago. McCurley was charged with capital murder, to which he pleaded not guilty.

McCurley's trial was held in August 2021. On the third day of the trial, he changed his plea to guilty and was sentenced to life in prison. Investigators believe McCurley may have been involved in the rapes and murders of several other young women in the Fort Worth area in the 1970s and 1980s, although he has not been charged with any additional crimes. He was imprisoned in Gib Lewis Unit and would have been eligible for parole on March 21, 2029, but died on July 15, 2023.

The breakthrough in Carla Walker's long-unsolved murder case offers a beacon of hope for me in the Witt case. The key that solved Carla's case—genealogy DNA testing—underscores the potential of even the smallest DNA samples in cracking cold cases. In Melissa Witt's investigation, the presence of DNA evidence, no matter how limited, represents a crucial piece of the puzzle that I believe will one day lead to a significant breakthrough.

This parallel between the two cases highlights the evolving landscape of forensic science and its growing ability to provide answers years, or even decades, after a crime has occurred. It reinforces the importance of preserving evidence and continually applying advancements in DNA technology to unsolved cases. The resolution of Carla Walker's case not only brings justice for her and her family but also renews hope for countless other cases awaiting their turn for closure. It also serves as a testament to the enduring commitment of investigators and the powerful impact of forensic advancements in the ongoing quest for justice.

Chapter 19: All the Lost Girls

Our decision to launch a nonprofit in Melissa Witt's honor was both low-key and monumental. As we shared cheese dip and drinks at our favorite Mexican restaurant, my best friend and fellow advocate Amy Smith and I discussed our future. We both agreed that our dream was to leave a legacy for Melissa while also serving the families of other murder victims.

Our experience in serving families with missing loved ones, combined with our passion for the Melissa Witt case, made this new pursuit an easy decision. As we chatted about our goals and dreams, we roughly mapped out our ideas on a paper napkin. Our mission: to build and improve awareness, resources, training and assistance for cold cases in the United States that meet our criteria of finding justice for female strangulation victims. And our agency would be dedicated to the memory of Melissa Ann Witt.

Confident we were on the right track, I looked up at Amy and said, "Now, we just need a name." As soon as I uttered those words, Melissa Witt, Laney Gwinner, and the faces of dozens of young women whose lives had been stolen suddenly surfaced.

Next I recalled 20-year-old Virginia Tech student Morgan Dana Harrington who attended a concert in Charlottesville, Virginia and never made it home.

On the evening of October 17, 2009, Harrington and three of her friends drove to the John Paul Jones Arena at the University of Virginia in Charlottesville to attend a Metallica concert.

During the opening act's performance, Morgan left her friends to use the restroom. When she did not return, they called her cell phone at 8:48 p.m. She told them that she was stuck outside the arena after she was denied re-entry by security guards at the exit.

During the call, Morgan told them not to worry and assured them she would find a ride back to Harrisonburg on her own, about an hour away.

The next day, October 18, 2009, Morgan's parents filed a missing person report when she did not show up at her their home to study with her father for a math exam.

That same day, Morgan's purse containing her identification and battery-less cell phone was discovered in the overflow parking lot of the university's Lannigan Athletic Field.

Investigators soon discovered that multiple witnesses on both sides of the Copeley Road bridge reported seeing a woman matching Morgan's description hitchhiking at around 9:30 pm that evening.

Shortly after Morgan's disappearance, I met her parents in Washington D.C. for dinner. Their story was heart-wrenching, and the pain on their faces as they made a plea for help in their daughter's disappearance is burned into my mind forever. Despite everyone's best efforts, this story did not have a happy ending. Exactly one hundred days after Morgan's disappearance, a farmer found her skeletonized remains in a remote pasture about six miles away from the concert venue.

That day, I was standing inside a Toys R Us department store when my phone rang. It was Morgan's father, Dan. "LaDonna," he stammered. "They found my girl. They found her remains in a field."

I gasped.

"What? Where?" I asked gently.

"A landowner driving a tractor through a hay field on his 700-acre farm in Albemarle County, Virginia, about ten miles from the John Paul Jones Arena, found her."

I was in utter shock. How could this be the ending to Morgan Harrington's story? Dan's words made me dizzy and my knees felt weak. As hot tears slid down my face, I slumped against a nearby shelf lined with smiling plastic dolls and wept.

This memory spilled immediately into that of Polly Hannah Klaas. I met her father, Marc Klaas, on that same trip to Washington D.C. in January of 2010. There, he told me about his 12-year-old daughter, Polly, who was abducted at knifepoint during a slumber party at her mother's home in Petaluma, California. Two months later, Polly's lifeless body was recovered. She had been strangled.

Next, the sweet face of JonBenet Ramsey surfaced. Sadly, six-year-old JonBenet was found murdered in her own home in December of 1996. The autopsy report stated that her official cause of death was "asphyxia by strangulation associated with craniocerebral trauma." Her case, often referred to as a national obsession, remains unsolved.

∽

As the dozens of young women who are missing or who have been murdered flooded my mind, it dawned on me: "All the Lost Girls," I blurted out.

"All the Lost Girls," Amy repeated as she nodded in agreement. "That's it. That's the perfect name."

Over the next few months, with the assistance of a local attorney, Amy and I filed the necessary paperwork to establish All the Lost Girls as an official nonprofit. Less than six weeks after that, our dream became a reality when the IRS approved our application. We immediately hit the ground running, launching a large-scale public awareness campaign to bring attention to Melissa Witt's unsolved murder. We sent out hundreds of press releases, hosted a press conference, and purchased 14 billboards in Arkansas to highlight Melissa's cold case.

Our work is incredibly important because the absence of a statute of limitations for violent crimes opens the door for cold cases to be revisited and potentially solved, even after many years have passed. Advances in forensic technology, particularly in DNA analysis, have revolutionized the way investigators approach these long-dormant cases, offering new hope for uncovering the truth and achieving justice.

The reality of the fact that law enforcement agencies are primarily focused on investigating and solving current crimes can indeed make it challenging to allocate resources and attention to cold cases. The passage of time not only dims the immediacy of these cases but also complicates investigative efforts due to the degradation of physical evidence and the fading memories of witnesses. In the immediate aftermath of a crime, the collection of evidence and testimonies is more straightforward, and the element of surprise can be a significant advantage in questioning suspects. However, as months and years go by, the trail often goes cold, leading to cases being shelved when all leads have been exhausted.

This is where All the Lost Girls plays a crucial role. By focusing on cold cases involving female strangulation victims, we help shine a light on cases that may have slipped through the cracks or fallen out of public consciousness. The specialized funding provided by our nonprofit earmarked for DNA testing, genetic genealogy, billboards, and other vital investigative resources breathes new life into these investigations, offering hope for breakthroughs and closure.

Moreover, the educational resources offered by All the Lost Girls serves a dual purpose: We not only raise awareness about the dangers of domestic abuse, stalking, human trafficking, and sexual assault but also empower survivors and potential victims with knowledge and strategies for protection and resilience. Through these efforts, we not only aid in the pursuit of justice for cold case victims but also contribute to the broader ongoing fight against violence and victimization of women.

Since day one, our fight for justice on behalf of Melissa Witt, and ultimately all the lost girls, has been relentless. And we will *never* give up.

Chapter 20: Mary Ann Witt

Over the years, I have amassed a comprehensive collection of newspaper and magazine articles, photos, and videos, along with thousands of pages of personally hand-written notes on the Witt case. Each piece of information has provided a deep insight into the intricacies of the investigation and the heart-wrenching impact it has had on those involved. Among the myriad of narratives, the accounts that detail the pain and suffering endured by Melissa's mother, Mary Ann Witt, stand out as the one thing that is the most difficult for me to absorb.

The resilience and enduring sorrow of a parent grappling with such an unimaginable loss brings a sobering human dimension to a case, far beyond the cold facts and figures often associated with criminal investigations. The stories of Mary Ann's perseverance in the face of such adversity, her relentless quest for justice, and her unwavering love for Melissa serve as a poignant reminder of the profound, lasting effects of violent crime on victims' families.

One of those reminders can be found within the pages of the various newspaper articles I have tucked safely away in the top drawer of my desk. When I open the pages to revisit the story, I am immediately confronted by a heartrending image of Melissa's mother, Mary Ann. The beautiful photo captures more than just a single moment in time; it encapsulates a mother's unwavering resolve and the undying hope that justice will prevail for her beloved only daughter. The title of the first article, "The Search for Justice: Slain Woman's Mother Keeps Hope Alive," not only speaks volumes about Mary Ann's relentless pursuit of answers and her refusal to let Melissa's memory fade into obscurity, but it also ignites a collective determination for both law enforcement and my team to seek justice for Melissa.

That article, written by John T. Anderson, and published by the *Times Record* on July 28, 2002, offers a heart-wrenching glimpse into the enduring agony of Mary Ann Witt over her loss. Mary Ann's words, "Melissa fought very hard," echo the unimaginable struggle that unfolded in the parking lot on that fateful day. "I believe she was unconscious when she left that parking lot…. I'm praying she died in that parking lot." Her hope that Melissa was unconscious, perhaps to spare her further pain, and her prayer that her daughter's suffering ended swiftly, reveal a profound depth of maternal despair.

The article further delves into the daily torment that Mary Ann experienced, describing a routine steeped in the painful ritual of reading newspapers and watching news reports about abducted children across the country. Mary Ann was constantly searching for answers, and hoping against hope that some clue might emerge that would shed light on who killed Melissa.

Another article in the *Times Record*, this one written by Amy Sherrill, shares the constant presence Melissa held in Mary Ann's daily life after her passing. The article poignantly captures a mother's struggle to navigate life in the wake of her child's absence. It also highlighted the personal and intimate ways in which individuals process grief, and the strength they muster to face each day, despite the void left behind. Mary Ann's story, as captured by Sherrill, is a reminder of the resilience of the human spirit in the face of ongoing sorrow, and the profound love that continues to bind loved ones, transcending even death.

As I revisit the news stories, each one a mosaic piece of the tragic narrative surrounding Melissa's murder, I feel a deep sense of sorrow. As a mother myself, my capacity to empathize with Mary Ann stems from an intrinsic understanding of the unconditional love and indescribable bond shared between a mother and her child.

A profound quote from Mary Ann Witt, featured in Marcus Blair's February 1999 article in the *Southwest Times Record*, touches on a complex and deeply emotional aspect of seeking justice in the aftermath of a horrific crime like this. "It's hard to say. When you've had a child murdered, I don't know if there can be closure. But I guess to get someone behind bars, it would bring me pleasure to know he's not out there to stalk other girls. Numerous lives would be saved."

Mary Ann Witt's selfless perspective on seeking justice serves as a profound source of inspiration. I admire the fact that her focus extended far beyond her own personal loss and need for closure to a broader, altruistic concern for the safety and well-being of others. This shift in narrative from individual grief to collective protection resonates deeply within me, and fuels my motivation to continue the fight for justice, not only in Melissa's case but in all cases where innocent lives are at stake or have been harmed. It reminds me that the pursuit of justice serves a dual purpose: providing some measure of peace to those directly affected while also upholding the broader principles of safety and morality within society.

One afternoon in the quiet of the Fort Smith Police Department conference room, I posed a sincere and heartfelt question to Jay C. Rider, Chris Boyd, and Detective Brad Marion. "Are we doing the right thing here?" I asked. "Is this what Mary Ann Witt wanted? Justice for Melissa at all costs?"

The question prompted a moment of introspection among the team, compelling each of us to quietly consider the profound impact of our work through the lens of a grieving mother's hopes and expectations. Suddenly, Jay C. Rider's confident and commanding voice pierced the heavy silence that had settled over the room. "Mary Ann wanted justice more than anything," Rider assured. "I promised her I would never give up until we had the killer behind bars. I know that Mary Ann would be proud of our efforts. And I have no doubt she would support us whole-heartedly if she were alive today. And that is one of the many reasons I won't give up." Rider looked around the room and added, "None of us should give up."

Rider's words reaffirmed our work while also serving as a rallying cry, reminding the team of our shared commitment for justice. This goal fuels our fierce determination to ensure that every lead is followed, every piece of evidence is scrutinized, and every possible avenue to uncover the truth is explored. The certainty in his voice also provided new meaning to our mission: Not only are we seeking justice for a 19-year-old murder victim, but we are also aiding in the fulfillment of a solemn vow made to her mother.

Even the otherwise stoic Detective Marion was visibly impacted by Rider's words. His demeanor changed and his facial expression shifted to an unmistakable look of determination. Moments after Rider spoke, Marion lifted his gaze from the meticulous notes on the desk in front of him and, in tune with the rhythmic tapping of his pen, he announced, "Justice *is* coming."

Detective Marion's words conveyed an unwavering conviction that served as inspiration for everyone in the room. But it was what Marion said next that shifted the atmosphere from one of reflection to one of action: "Now, let's do everything in our power to make this happen!"

The sincerity of his directive brought a renewed focus and energy to the team—reinforcing the shared purpose that united us: to bring closure to Melissa Witt's case and deliver on the promise of justice, not only for her, but also for her mother and for all those who have been touched by the tragedy of this brutal crime.

Chapter 21: Detective Brad Marion

Detective Brad Marion's journey from his early life in Alma, Arkansas, to becoming a key figure in the Fort Smith Police Department's detective division is a narrative of dedication, passion, and a deep-seated commitment to public service. Born in Fort Smith and raised in Alma, Marion's upbringing in the area grounded him in the community he would later serve.

He initially pursued an EMT/Paramedic license at ATU-Ozark. His trajectory toward a career dedicated to public service and safety was cemented in this foundational commitment to helping others in critical situations—a trait that would later seamlessly translate into his career in law enforcement.

Marion would go on to gain experience as a 911 dispatcher for the Crawford County Sheriff's Office—a pursuit that was instrumental in shaping his understanding of law enforcement and emergency response. In this role, Marion not only learned the importance of quick thinking and calmness under pressure but he also deepened his appreciation for the complexities and challenges faced by first responders. It was in this position he learned the value of coordinating with various emergency services, understanding the urgency and severity of different situations, and providing a crucial link between the public and the assistance they require.

This early exposure to the front lines of emergency response also provided him with a unique perspective on public safety, equipping him with skills and insights that would later prove invaluable in his subsequent role as the lead detective in Melissa Witt's unsolved murder. And it was this foundational experience that formed the bedrock for what has proven to be a successful career in public service.

One afternoon, as Detective Marion and I sat down to discuss both his life and his law enforcement aspirations, he explained that his participation in ride-alongs marked a pivotal moment in his career. "Ride-alongs gave me firsthand insights into the day-to-day realities of law enforcement," he said, leaning back in his chair. "That experience gave me a tangible sense of the challenges and rewards associated with police work. That hands-on training and education became vividly real for me and fostered a deeper appreciation for the complexities of the job requirements."

His transition to the patrol division in 2007 was a natural progression for Marion. Patrolling, with its dynamic and varied nature, offered him the opportunity to directly engage with the community he serves, responding to incidents in real time, while making important contributions to public safety. This role undoubtedly honed his skills in quick decision-making, situational assessment, and effective communication—all crucially valuable attributes for a law enforcement officer.

It was his hands-on experience in the patrol division, however, that would further solidify his commitment to the profession. His direct interaction with the public, and the firsthand encounters with the challenges they face, gave Marion the opportunity to provide immediate assistance that not only helped maintain public safety and order, but also saved lives.

This period of Marion's career played a key role in shaping his approach to policing, and led to him joining the Fort Smith Police Department (FSPD) in 2018. There, Marion quickly advanced to the detective division and then to the crimes against persons unit. In my interviews with Brad Marion's peers and supervisors, it became evident that he is esteemed highly within the law enforcement community. This widespread respect is indicative of Marion's professionalism, dedication, and the positive effect he has had on his colleagues.

My experience working with Marion on the Melissa Witt case echoes those sentiments. He embodies the qualities essential for effective law enforcement: integrity, empathy, and resilience. He leads by example, works collaboratively, and has a willingness to go above and beyond in his duties in a commitment to find justice.

When Marion took over the investigation into Melissa Witt's unsolved murder, he quickly learned that it was a significant responsibility that required a new kind of dedication to seeking justice for victims, their families, and the public at large—and there is absolutely no doubt that he successfully met that challenge head on. His path from a young man in Alma to a dedicated detective in Fort Smith is remarkable. As I've gotten to know him over the years, I've grown to admire how deeply invested he is in the welfare of his community. But his pursuit of justice in Melissa Witt's case is something I respect more than anything. Marion embodies the perseverance and tenacity required to work on a cold case, where leads can be scarce and the passage of time adds layers of complexity. His dedication serves as a beacon of hope for those of us who are awaiting answers in Melissa's unsolved murder. Most importantly, Marion demonstrates the profound impact that committed individuals can have in the quest for justice.

Detective Brad Marion's connection to the 1995 abduction of Morgan Nick adds a fascinating and poignant layer to both his personal and professional life. Being present at the ballpark as a little league player during the event that led to one of the most high-profile abduction cases in Arkansas not only ties him personally to a pivotal moment in the community's history but also provides him with a unique insight into the emotional and societal impact of such tragedies.

His direct link to the Morgan Nick case instills in Marion a deeply personal motivation to solve cold cases, underpinned by an acute understanding of the pain and uncertainty that lingers in the wake of unresolved abductions. It's a connection that transcends the professional realm, touching on the core of human empathy and the intrinsic desire for justice.

The abduction of Morgan Nick has haunted the small town of Alma, Arkansas, and the entire nation, since 1995. On the evening of June 9, 1995, Morgan, a spirited six-year-old girl, attended a little league baseball game with her mother, Colleen Nick, at a local ballpark. More than a game it was a place where families and friends came together to enjoy America's favorite pastime and the company of one another.

As the game unfolded, Morgan and some friends were drawn to the innocent childhood pleasure of catching lightning bugs near the parking lot. This seemingly mundane activity took a tragic turn when, at approximately 10:45 p.m., Morgan suddenly vanished. Her friends reported that they had seen a man talking to Morgan near her mother's car while she was emptying sand out of her shoes.

The police were alerted, and a massive search operation was launched immediately. The community of Alma, the state of Arkansas, and, eventually, the entire country were gripped by the urgency of finding the young girl.

The abduction of Morgan Nick, occurring six months after the murder of Melissa Witt, presented a chilling timeline within the community, marking a period fraught with fear, uncertainty, and grief. These back-to-back tragedies compounded the community's sense of vulnerability, and the proximity in timing between these two cases initially led investigators to explore potential connections between the two crimes. While no direct link was established between Melissa Witt and Morgan Nick, the parallel events left an indelible mark on the community.

Marion's personal ties to Morgan Nick's unresolved abduction serves as a powerful motivator in his investigative work, infusing his approach with a deep sense of purpose and commitment. This personal connection to a significant event in his community has also instilled in him an unwavering dedication to solving Melissa Witt's case.

There is an "invisible string of connection" that ties Detective Brad Marion to both the abduction of Morgan Nick and the murder of Melissa Witt—a connection that has shaped not only his approach to investigative work, but has also deepened his resolve. It has also created a unique bond between Marion, Rider, Boyd, and me.

This shared connection fosters a sense of solidarity and mutual understanding, rooted in a common goal of seeking justice and resolution for Melissa Witt. It has created a partnership driven by a shared emotional investment in the outcome of this case. It has also given birth to a collaboration where community members, law enforcement officers, and advocates come together united by their personal ties and professional expertise. It's a testament to the idea that personal experiences and connections can significantly influence and enrich the work of solving a complex case like Melissa's. It has brought together diverse perspectives and skills in the shared mission of uncovering the truth.

Marion's commitment to Melissa Witt's case, despite the constraints imposed by his substantial caseload, is a testament to his dedication and resolve. Last year alone, he was assigned 367 cases; yet, his ability to investigate those crimes and still allocate time to Melissa's unsolved murder speaks to his profound desire to bring closure to this long-unsolved mystery.

The faith I have in Marion's investigative skills, combined with his unwavering personal commitment to a 19-year-old girl that he never knew, convinces me that he will be the detective, after almost three decades, to push this case to the finish line. "It's going to be you," I said to him one afternoon on the phone. "You are going to solve this case."

"I am giving it my all. And I will not stop until we know who killed Melissa Witt," he promised me.

I whole-heartedly believe him.

Chapter 22: Dale Best

Sixteen years before Brad Marion was born, Dale Best began his impressive career in law enforcement. Beginning his journey right out of high school in 1970, Dale's early roles as a file clerk and fingerprint technician with the FBI provided him with the foundational knowledge and experience that would shape his future in law enforcement. His transition to a radio operator at the Sebastian County Sheriff's Office marked the beginning of his deep involvement in local law enforcement efforts.

In 1972, Dale's career took a significant turn when he joined the Arkansas State Police (ASP) as a Tel/Comm Operator in Fort Smith. This role not only expanded his technical skills but also deepened his understanding of the intricacies of police communication and operations. His dedication to serving his community and country was further demonstrated when he joined the Arkansas Army National Guard as a medic, showcasing his commitment to public service in multiple capacities.

Dale's time at the ASP saw him take on the challenging role of an Undercover Narcotics Investigator, a position that demanded not only a high degree of bravery and discretion but also a keen understanding of the drug trade and its impact on communities. His subsequent transfer to the Highway Patrol Division as a Trooper in 1976 allowed him to gain invaluable experience in patrol duties and traffic enforcement, further broadening his law enforcement expertise.

In 1979, Best transferred into the Criminal Division as an Undercover Investigator stationed in Washington County, Arkansas. This marked a return to covert operations, where Dale's skills in undercover work were put to significant use. His promotion to Sergeant in 1982 then to Lieutenant in 1986 gave him the opportunity to take on leadership roles, such as supervising undercover investigations across a vast 12-county area in Northwest Arkansas. These positions required not only investigative acumen but also strong leadership and organizational skills.

As a Lieutenant and Company Commander, Best's impressive leadership expanded to overseeing 15 Criminal Investigators and a civilian employee, while also managing both overt and covert investigations. In 1995, the year Melissa Witt's body was found in the Ozark National Forest, Best received a promotion to Captain and Troop Commander of Troop H in Fort Smith. His responsibilities encompassed all Highway Patrol activities and Arkansas Driver license examinations in a five-county area. On January 13, 1995 Dale Best, along with Jay C. Rider, Chris Boyd, and the former Sebastian County Prosecutor, Ron

Fields, were among the first on the scene when two animal trappers found Melissa's body on logging road 1551 in Franklin County. Years later, Best would confide in me that that day was one of the worst in his career. "I held in all my emotions the best that I could," he explained. "But it was devastating for all of us that Melissa's story ended that way."

In 1997, Best's career culminated in his promotion to the Commander of the Criminal Investigation Division in Little Rock, where he led a substantial team of 256 commissioned and civilian personnel. This highlighted his extensive experience, leadership, and dedication to law enforcement across the state of Arkansas.

Upon retiring in 1999, Dale Best left behind a legacy of service, leadership, and commitment to law enforcement that not only impacted the Arkansas State Police but also set a high standard for future generations in the field. His career, a remarkable example of lifelong dedication to public service and community safety did not end there, however. After his illustrious career with the Arkansas State Police, Dale Best transitioned to a significant role with the Drug Enforcement Administration (DEA), which he held from 2002 to 2007, further extending his influential career in law enforcement. As the Intelligence Research Specialist for Arkansas, Best played a crucial role in supporting the DEA's mission to combat drug trafficking and drug-related crimes within the state and beyond.

In this capacity, he provided both tactical and strategic support to federal agents of the DEA, leveraging his extensive background in narcotics investigation and law enforcement intelligence. His work involved analyzing complex data, identifying patterns and trends in drug trafficking, and developing actionable intelligence that would aid in the planning and execution of DEA operations. The insights and expertise Dale brought to this role were invaluable in enhancing the effectiveness of drug enforcement strategies and operations.

Best's contributions to the DEA during this time underscored his deep commitment to public service and his unwavering dedication to combating the scourge of illegal drugs. His role required not only a sophisticated understanding of drug trafficking networks and their operations but also the ability to work collaboratively with federal agents and other law enforcement partners to achieve common goals.

Unfortunately, Best's tenure with the DEA came to a close in 2007 when he retired due to health issues. His retirement marked the end of a distinguished career in law enforcement that spanned several decades and allowed him to make significant contributions to the safety and security of his community and country.

Ten years after his retirement, I reached out to Best and asked him to discuss his involvement in the Melissa Witt investigation. His legacy, built on a foundation of dedication, bravery, and a relentless pursuit of justice, made him an invaluable source of knowledge, particularly in a case as complex and long-standing as Melissa's.

Best was more than willing to discuss everything with me, despite the years that had passed since his active duty.

His insights into the investigative strategies, the evolution of the case, and the inherent challenges in solving Melissa's murder offered a unique perspective that enriched my ongoing efforts to find justice for Melissa and her family.

The connection formed that afternoon evolved into a fast friendship—a testament to the shared resolve and emotional commitment in seeing justice served. My friendship with Best served as a poignant reminder that behind every cold case are not only the unseen faces of the victims and their waiting families but also a community of dedicated professionals who carry these cases with them, long after the files are closed for the day. His unshakeable desire to see Melissa's killer brought to justice mirrored the sentiments of Rider, Boyd, and Marion. This camaraderie and shared dedication in the pursuit of answers in cold cases like Melissa's is a beautiful example of how a collective effort that spans across years and careers can unite a varied group of individuals in the common goal of uncovering the truth.

One evening, as we delved into the intricate web of possibilities and theories surrounding Melissa Witt's case, Best and I discussed everything from local rumors to the numerous violent offenders interviewed and the myriad of paths the case had taken over the years. "She knew her killer," Best offered up unexpectedly. I carefully considered his words. It was interesting to learn that he shared the same sentiments that the other investigators held in the Witt case. His words played on repeat in my head: "She knew her killer." Statistically, this betrayal of trust is a common thread in so many cases, where the perpetrator is not a stranger but someone within the victim's orbit—a chilling reminder of the potential dangers lurking within familiar circles.

"Do you think his name was in her diary?" I asked.

"Oh definitely," he replied, his voice trailing off.

The mention of Melissa Witt's diary, a seemingly innocuous detail, struck a chord with Best, stirring a memory that had lain dormant in the depths of his experience with the case. As his voice trailed off, it was clear that this recollection was more than just a fleeting thought; it was a significant piece of the puzzle that he was considering as he replayed the vast expanse of the investigation in his mind.

"I interviewed someone once," he said slowly. "I never could shake the feeling I had about him. I always wondered if he might be involved in her murder," Best confided.

"Can you tell me what you remember about him?" I asked.

"I can tell you his name," Best answered. I closed my eyes, bracing myself for Best's reply. In my heart, I already knew what he was going to say. And as he gave me the name of our unnamed suspect, my stomach churned and a wave of emotions washed over me. This pivotal exchange represented a critical juncture in my investigation into Melissa Witt's case, aligning my independent suspicions with Best's experienced insights.

The silence that hung in the air as I processed Best's confirmation naturally piqued his investigator instincts

"You do not seem surprised by this revelation," he observed. His keen ability to read reactions, a skill honed over years of law enforcement experience, was as strong as it had ever been. "Do you know him?" he asked, cutting to the core of the matter.

"He's been in contact with me," I replied.

"Of course he has," Best offered, his voice marked by a slow and confident delivery. His tone revealed a seasoned investigator's intuition and understanding of the complexities that surrounded the reasons behind our unnamed suspect's contact with me.

"A suspect interjecting himself into an investigation is not uncommon, particularly those that remain unsolved for extended periods of time," Best explained. "This behavior is driven by a variety of motives, including a desire to gauge how much the investigators know, an attempt to control the narrative, or even a compulsion to relive their crime," Best continued. "Rider knows?" he asked.

"He knows," I answered.

"Good," he responded. "This is good."

Not long after that call, Best's health took a turn for the worse, and the nature of our interactions shifted. The focus of our conversations moved away from the intricacies of the Melissa Witt case to more personal reflections on his life, his family, and the remarkable journey he had taken throughout his law enforcement career. I enjoyed discussing his rich history. It provided me a chance to honor and acknowledge the breadth of his contributions, not only to specific cases like Melissa Witt's but to the broader field of law enforcement. It was also an opportunity to celebrate the man behind the badge, his values, the sacrifices he made, and the impact he had on his community and colleagues. Looking back, I hope these conversations provided comfort and a sense of legacy for Best, knowing that his life's work resonated with others and would be remembered.

Before his death in 2019, I received an email from him. "Hi friend. I think about you and I care about your safety. Be careful with the Witt case. That man who calls you could be the one. Always stop and smell the flowers and enjoy the butterflies," he wrote. He signed the email, "Your friend, Dale Best."

This final message, despite the evident impact of his health condition on his ability to communicate, underscored the connection that had formed between us—one that transcended the professional realm and had entered into genuine friendship.

Sadly, Dale Best passed away on January 24, 2019. He was only 66 years old. His passing marked the end of a remarkable career in law enforcement and the loss of a true friend and ally in the quest for justice. His legacy and the impact of his friendship, however, continue to resonate with me, serving as a reminder of the enduring power of human connection.

A week after he passed away, I drove to Fort Smith to pay my respects to Melissa Witt. As I approached her graveside, I discovered a small piece of paper tucked neatly into a pink bouquet adorning her final resting place. On the page was an intricately drawn butterfly, hand-painted in the colors of black, blue, white, and gold.

Tears welled in my eyes as I placed the beautiful drawing back into the delicate flower arrangement. This discovery just a week after Best's passing felt like a serendipitous echo of Dale Best's final email to me. The symbolic gesture, whether left by someone inspired by the same message or sheer coincidence, beautifully encapsulated his message to me to appreciate the simple joys and wonders of life. It was as if, through this small but significant token, Best's spirit and his final words were reaching out, reminding me to hold on to the light even in the darkest of investigations.

Chapter 23: Butterflies

A year after Dale Best passed away, I invited my husband to accompany my documentary team as we ventured back into the Ozark National Forest. This expedition was centered around our goal of completing the filming for the documentary on the Melissa Witt case.

For my husband, Danny, this visit to the Ozark National Forest was an immersion into a setting of stark contrasts. On one hand, the natural beauty of the national park, with its expansive vistas, dense woodlands, and serene waterways, presented a breathtaking tableau of the natural world at its most majestic and serene. The Ozarks, renowned for their rugged beauty, offer a tranquil refuge and a reminder of the enduring splendor of the natural world.

Yet, this awe-inspiring backdrop was juxtaposed with a somber reality—the knowledge that these very woods were the final resting place of Melissa Witt, where her life was tragically and prematurely taken. This realization imbued the visit with a profound sense of sadness, reminding us of the fragility of life and the devastating impact of senseless acts of violence. The forest, while beautiful, also stood as a silent witness to a profound loss, adding a layer of solemnity to the team's mission.

This emotional dichotomy—marveling at the forest's beauty while grappling with the tragedy it harbored—highlighted the delicate balance between capturing the essence of the case and honoring the memory of Melissa, all while navigating the personal effect such a journey entails.

As my team unloaded our equipment, the forest, with all its beauty and sorrow, stood as a powerful symbol of the documentary's purpose: to shed light on Melissa's story, to seek answers, and to ensure that, amidst the majesty of nature, her voice and her story are not forgotten.

The sudden landing of a large, ornate butterfly on our equipment amidst the solemn task of filming Melissa Witt's story was a moment of unexpected wonder. The butterfly, with its impressive size and stunning beauty, seemed out of place yet perfectly timed, as if nature itself was reaching out during a moment of deep reflection and purposefulness.

The butterfly, with its intricate patterns and vibrant hues, stood in stark contrast to the somber backdrop of logging road 1551, transforming the space into an exhibition of life's fragile balance between beauty and sorrow. Without warning, the butterfly took flight, and its sudden departure, much like its arrival, served as a reminder of the ephemeral nature of beauty and the transient moments that punctuate our lives and endeavors.

As the butterfly disappeared into the expanse of the Ozark National Forest, it seemed to symbolize the delicate dance between presence and absence, between the tangible and the ethereal.

Minutes after my team returned to our task of filming, the butterfly reappeared, gently circling overhead before eventually landing on the tombstone-like rock where Melissa Witt's body had once been hidden away. The butterfly seemed to be conveying a message from nature itself—acknowledging our efforts to bring Melissa's story to light.

We watched on as the butterfly launched into the air and began circling overhead before delicately landing on my hand. I let out a small gasp as this already poignant moment transformed into one of profound significance for my team. Our collective awe at this gentle interaction with nature, particularly in the context of our work on the documentary, pulled us into deeper reflection on the connections between our endeavors and the world around us.

This moment of connection, with the butterfly choosing to land so trustingly on my hand, felt like an affirmation of Melissa's presence and influence on our team, a reminder that her story and spirit are integral to our work. Later, I would learn that in many cultures, butterflies are seen as exactly that—messengers from the spirit world—symbols of transformation and rebirth.

As I stared at the butterfly's colors and patterns, I quickly realized that they mirrored the drawing found at Melissa's graveside. This felt like more than just mere coincidence. For the first time, it was as if we had a tangible link to Melissa, a visual echo of her memory manifesting in the here and now.

As the butterfly took flight for the final time, its wings beating softly against the backdrop of the Ozark National Forest, the moment encapsulated a profound sense of connection and renewal. The experience, marked by awe and a deepened resolve, underscored the powerful impact of such serendipitous encounters, especially in the context of a project as emotionally charged and significant as our investigative documentary on Melissa Witt.

This encounter with the butterfly, so intricately tied to Melissa through the drawing at her graveside and now its physical presence, seemed to represent the young girl whose life and story I am so dedicated to illuminating. The beauty and grace of the butterfly, fleeting yet powerful, a reminder of the beauty and potential that was lost but also of the enduring effect she continues to have.

The awe and renewed strength I felt as the butterfly departed symbolized a recommitment to the cause, a reminder of the importance of the work my team is undertaking. It was an incredible manifestation of the connection between Melissa's memory and our ongoing quest for justice and understanding. In that moment, the butterfly became a symbol of hope and resilience.

Years after the memorable encounter with the butterfly in the Ozark National Forest, another poignant moment unfolded, this time in an unexpected locale—Heathrow

International Airport in the UK. Far removed from the serene natural backdrop of the Ozarks, the bustling environment of one of the world's busiest airports became the stage for the next significant sign related to the Melissa Witt case.

Standing amid the constant flow of travelers, the sounds of announcements, and the whirl of activity that defines an international airport, I found myself overwhelmed. My journey to London, to share Melissa's story across continents at CrimeCon UK, was a testament to the depth of my commitment to shedding light on her case. Yet, standing in one of the world's largest airports, the enormity of the task ahead sparked a moment of self-doubt. The responsibility of doing justice to Melissa's story, especially so far from home, weighed heavily on my heart.

As I stood alone in the airport, entrenched in a whirlwind of emotions, something unexpected happened. A familiar face suddenly appeared in the sea of strangers. It was Levi Risely, a former detective on Melissa's case. Our coincidental meeting in the UK, both there for entirely different reasons and without prior knowledge of each other's travel plans, was a remarkable occurrence.

Seeing him at that very moment seemed almost fated. Much like the butterfly's appearance in the Ozark National Forest, Risley's presence in such an unexpected place provided a tangible connection to Melissa, grounding me in the moment and dispelling my rising tide of doubt.

I interpreted this encounter, seemingly by chance, as a sign of reassurance, echoing the sentiment of the butterfly's visit. Risley's presence in London, whether by coincidence or design, became a symbol of continuity and support, reinforcing our shared dedication to uncovering the truth and seeking justice for Melissa.

As I exited the airport to catch the train to my hotel, I was unknowingly set on a path toward an interaction that would carry its own significance. As I grabbed a seat on the train, the woman next to me smiled and said hello. This simple gesture of warmth and openness sparked a conversation that transformed a routine transit into a moment of genuine human connection. Our small talk, casual yet significant in its own right, served as reinforcement of the day's earlier experiences, reminding me of the support and solidarity that can be found in unexpected places. The coincidence of her first name also being Melissa could not be missed. However, it became more than that.

As we arrived at her stop, my new friend and I exchanged business cards in hopes of transforming our fleeting encounter into a potential lasting friendship. After she exited the train and we waved goodbye, I glanced down at her card. Her business logo took my breath away. It was decorated with a butterfly motif in the colors of black, blue, and gold. The presence of this butterfly mirrored the earlier encounter in the Ozark National Forest and the drawing I found at Melissa Witt's graveside. The recurring theme of the butterfly, appearing at pivotal moments in my work on the Melissa Witt case, began to weave a compelling narrative, rich in symbolism and connection.

The exchange of a simple business card underscored the idea that even in the vast tapestry of human experiences, there are threads that bind us together, often revealed in the most surprising of ways.

Chapter 24: CrimeCon Catalyst

In 2022, prior to my trip to CrimeCon in the UK, my journey through the intricate maze of the Melissa Witt case took an unexpected yet pivotal turn when I found myself amidst the buzz and fervor of CrimeCon U.S. This gathering, a mecca for true crime aficionados, experts, and narrators from around the globe, was not merely an event; it was the epicenter of a movement driven by a collective thirst for truth and justice that propelled both my career and the Melissa Witt case into new realms of possibility and public awareness.

Attending CrimeCon wasn't initially on my radar. My journey into the depths of the Melissa Witt case had been a mostly solitary endeavor, fueled by a relentless pursuit of justice and a deep-seated need to tell her story. However, the chance to participate in CrimeCon presented an opportunity to elevate Melissa's case from the shadows of obscurity to the spotlight of the true crime community's collective consciousness.

The lead up to CrimeCon was a whirlwind of preparation and anticipation. Crafting my first book,

The Girl I Never Knew, was a journey through complex emotions and facts, a delicate balance between honoring Melissa's memory and presenting an unvarnished look at the realities of unsolved cases. The book aimed not just to tell a story but to connect readers with the essence of Melissa's life and the void her unsolved murder has left in the fabric of her community and beyond.

The reception at CrimeCon was beyond anything I anticipated. As I stood before a sea of faces, each person there shared a common thread of empathy, curiosity, and a hunger for justice. The connection was palpable, a shared energy that coursed through the room as I delved into the complexities of Melissa's case. Questions poured in, each one a testament to the audience's engagement and desire to contribute to the search for answers.

The book launch at CrimeCon exceeded all expectations. Attendees were not just passive listeners; they were engaged, inquisitive, and empathetic participants in a shared journey. The questions posed were insightful, reflecting a deep understanding of the complexities involved in cold cases and a genuine concern for the victims and their families. It was evident that *The Girl I Never Knew* resonated with many, bridging the gap between a name in a decades-old case file and the real, vibrant young woman Melissa once was.

The impact of the book's launch at such a significant venue reverberated far beyond the confines of the convention. Social media platforms lit up with discussions about the book and Melissa's case, leading to increased public interest, and, crucially, to new tips and leads. The visibility afforded by CrimeCon helped propel *The Girl I Never Knew* into the broader consciousness, making it not just a book but a catalyst for renewed investigative efforts and public engagement.

For me, the CrimeCon book launch was more than a milestone; it was a reaffirmation of the power of storytelling and community in the pursuit of justice. It underscored the importance of never losing sight of the human stories at the heart of true crime, and reinforced my commitment to ensuring that Melissa, the girl I never knew, would never be forgotten.

CrimeCon 2022 and the launch of *The Girl I Never Knew* epitomized the convergence of passion, advocacy, and action. It was a clear message to me that, in the realm of true crime, the pursuit of justice is a collective endeavor, one that requires the dedication of not just professionals but every one of us who believes in the power of truth and the necessity of remembering those we have lost.

Chapter 25: Uneven Ground: The Melissa Witt Story

Another significant milestone in the journey to bring Melissa Witt's story to a broader audience occurred when our film, *Uneven Ground: The Melissa Witt Story*, premiered on May 20, 2023 at True Crime Fest in Rogers, Arkansas, eight years after the inception of our documentary project.

We chose the title *Uneven Ground* as a metaphor for the complex and challenging terrain of the investigation, both literally, in the physical search for clues within diverse and rugged landscapes, and figuratively, in navigating the intricate web of leads, theories, and emotions that surround Melissa Witt's tragic disappearance and murder.

The documentary delves deep into Melissa's story, beginning with her life, her dreams, and the profound impact her loss had on her family, friends, and the broader community. It examines the initial investigation, highlighting the tireless efforts of law enforcement and the challenges they faced due to the limitations of forensic technology at the time and the elusive nature of the perpetrator.

The documentary is not just a recounting of a cold case. It is a testament to the human spirit's resilience, the relentless pursuit of truth, and the hope that, even in the face of adversity, justice can be achieved. It is a narrative that invites reflection, fosters empathy, and inspires a renewed commitment to uncovering the truth, ensuring that Melissa Witt's life and legacy are honored and remembered.

Shortly after the premiere, my team entered *Uneven Ground* into the film festival circuit. This was a strategic move in hopes of elevating the documentary's visibility and impact. Film festivals serve as crucial platforms for independent films to gain recognition, engage with broader audiences, and stimulate critical conversations around the subjects they explore.

We knew that by participating in the film festival circuit, our documentary would reach diverse audiences—everyone from industry professionals and critics to true crime enthusiasts and the general public. Each festival screening provides an opportunity to share Melissa Witt's story with new viewers, sparking discussions and potentially drawing fresh attention to her case.

The festival circuit also offers the chance to garner accolades and critical acclaim, further validating the importance of the documentary's subject matter and the quality of its production. Awards and positive reception can propel a film into more screenings, media coverage, and possibly even distribution deals, expanding its reach even further.

My team took a bold step and we entered *Uneven Ground: The Melissa Witt Story* into 75 film festivals. Entering such a vast number of festivals significantly impacted public awareness of Melissa's case, and, in turn, generated new information and leads.

Additionally, film festivals foster a community of filmmakers, advocates, and activists by providing a valuable network for collaboration, support, and the exchange of ideas. For us, this has led to new partnerships and projects, and further amplified the documentary's impact in the ongoing quest for justice in Melissa's case.

Our decision to enter *Uneven Ground* into the film festival circuit was not primarily driven by the pursuit of accolades. Most importantly, it represented our strategic and heartfelt effort to share her story. This approach reflected our documentary's deeper purpose: to resonate with audiences, inspire collective action, and contribute meaningfully to our quest for justice.

To our surprise, the film has (so far) received 25 awards. I attribute this honor to my team's hard work and dedication to shedding light on this deeply moving and complex mystery. These accolades not only honor the commitment of my team but also honor Melissa's memory.

The widespread recognition and success of *Uneven Ground,* evidenced by its availability on major platforms like Amazon Prime and Tubi, and the remarkable viewership of over 6 million people, is a testament to the profound impact Melissa's story has had on a global audience. The accessibility of the film on popular streaming platforms significantly broadens its reach, allowing individuals from various backgrounds and locations to engage with the story, which plays a crucial role in keeping the conversation around her case alive.

The first time I stood on that remote mountain top in the Ozark National Forest, it was a pivotal moment in my journey for justice for Melissa Witt. It was there, amidst the solemn beauty and quiet of nature, that I made a profound commitment—I vowed to find her killer and to keep her memory alive. This promise was deeply meaningful and went beyond mere investigative journalism or documentary filmmaking. It represented a personal crusade fueled by empathy, justice, and the desire to honor Melissa's life and legacy.

My resolve to keep Melissa's memory alive and to tirelessly seek answers in her case is the driving force behind all of my work. It has guided my efforts to navigate the complexities of this investigation, to engage with those who knew Melissa, and to piece together the narrative of her life and the tragic circumstances of her disappearance and murder. This commitment has also been my source of strength during challenging moments, reminding me of the importance of what I am doing and the impact it can have not just on solving Melissa's case, but on raising awareness about similar stories and the broader issues they highlight.

The promise to Melissa, made in the solitude of the Ozark National Forest, has set me on a path marked by determination, compassion, and a relentless pursuit of justice. As *Uneven Ground: The Melissa Witt Story* continues to be recognized and celebrated, it carries with it the hope that the spotlight on Melissa's case will not only honor her memory but also bring us closer to the resolution that Melissa, her family, and all who have been touched by her story so rightly deserve.

Chapter 26: Someone Knows

The surge in calls to our anonymous tipline following the documentary premiere was a testament to the significant effect *Uneven Ground* had in reigniting public interest and involvement in Melissa's case. Among the sea of tips, I noticed a pattern of a recurring hang-up call. And while it is not uncommon for an anonymous tipline to receive hang up calls, this situation seemed unique because I quickly identified a predictable pattern in the days and times that the calls were made. This recurring behavior suggested something more than random or accidental calls; it indicated a deliberate attempt to reach out, hinting at a potential internal battle the caller was experiencing.

The consistency in timing, I surmised, might reflect a specific period when the caller felt a stronger connection to Melissa's case or found themselves alone and able to call the tipline. Just before some of the calls disconnected, I could hear the sound of soft crying in the background. I wondered if this could be a possible indication of a deep emotional connection to the information they might hold. I knew from years of experience that this type of scenario is a perfect example of the complex psychological and emotional factors that can influence potential witnesses or individuals with crucial information. The fear of coming forward can be paralyzing for a tipster, especially if the information they possess could implicate someone they know—or even themselves. Additionally, guilt, either from withholding information or from involvement in the events surrounding the case, could exacerbate this paralysis, making the act of revealing what they know a profound internal struggle.

My challenge, then, was to create a pathway for this individual to come forward so they would feel safe and secure. To do this, I released a post on social media reassuring potential informants about the confidentiality and protective measures in place for the tipline. I also provided alternative methods of communication so they could convey the information that was clearly causing them a great deal of distress. My goal was to convert this cycle of hesitation and silence into a breakthrough that could provide critical leads in the investigation.

My hunch was right. Three days after my post, I received an email from the previously silent caller. The subject line of the email, marked by the plea, "Please Keep Me Anonymous" suggested a mix of fear, urgency, and a pressing need to share information while also protecting their identity. My heart raced as I considered the "why" behind their desperate need for confidentiality. Was their fear driven by concern over their own safety or that of their loved ones? Was it driven by their involvement in Melissa Witt's murder or with a suspect?

I took a deep breath and opened the email. As I scanned the words on the screen, I was startled to discover that the author revealed her connection to both Melissa Witt and the unnamed suspect. She described in detail firsthand observations of his violent and erratic behavior. "He hurts women," she wrote. "And he has absolutely no conscience. He will kill me if he finds out I sent this to you."

I carefully considered the gravity of the situation before crafting my response. The chilling description provided by the author aligned with previous allegations I had encountered about the suspect's dangerous nature, and this email reinforced the sense of urgency and importance of this lead in the investigation.

The author's vivid portrayal and the emotional weight behind her words made me pause, and my intuition urged me to navigate this territory delicately. My response included a request for "any other specific details." My hope was to encourage further dialogue without overwhelming or pressuring someone who was already very fearful. My goal was to open the door for her to share more about her experiences and observations, which could be crucial in piecing together a more comprehensive understanding of the suspect's behavior and his interactions with other young women.

Her immediate response left me speechless. Her email detailed how our unnamed suspect had stalked her for days by sitting in her office parking lot, watching her for hours at a time. The police were called and they issued a warning, but that did not stop the escalation of his actions. On the fourth day, like a predator ready to pounce on his prey, he slashed all four of her tires and left a note with the words, "Next time, it will be your throat." "His predilection for threatening and destructive behavior is frightening," I whispered to myself as I continued reading. "But I'm not the only one," she explained. "There are others that he did this to."

She went on to describe how our unnamed suspect stalked another woman in a mall parking lot. And then, according to the email, a violent confrontation ensued that resulted in him shoving the woman to the ground. The description of the encounter was deeply disturbing. The similarities between this account and the circumstances surrounding the Witt case were too striking to be ignored. Our suspect seemed to be operating under a specific modus operandi that involved targeting women in isolated parking areas.

This revelation not only reinforced the incredibly dangerous nature of the suspect but it also highlighted a potential pattern in his actions that could be crucial in linking him to Melissa Witt's murder. The fact that these incidents involved public, yet relatively isolated, spaces like parking lots, and quickly escalated to physical violence, caused me to pick up the phone and call Jay C. Rider.

I opened the call with, "He's our guy. I just know it."

There was a long pause before Rider spoke. "Did you find another victim?" he asked.

"Yes. Unfortunately," I answered.

The words we spoke next, in hushed whispers, centered on our unnamed suspect and our desire to see him held accountable for his crimes. We also agreed that the courage of the author to share these harrowing experiences, despite the evident risk to her own safety, was remarkable. We agreed it would be imperative for me to continue providing her with support and ensuring her protection. Her insights could also prove to be invaluable in painting a more comprehensive picture of the suspect's history and could also be the key to unlocking further leads in the pursuit of justice for Melissa Witt, and potentially other victims.

Confident in the plan we devised, I hung up with Rider. Seconds later, my phone alerted me to a comment left on the "Who Killed Missy Witt" Facebook page. The author had written the words, "I hate you for what you are doing. You have made a circus of the Witt case. I hate you." The words, jarring and hurtful, struck at the heart of my intentions and the endless work I've put into Melissa's case.

Upon closer inspection, I discovered the harsh comment came from someone within Melissa Witt's extended friend circle. This added a layer of complexity and personal betrayal to the situation. It was particularly disheartening to receive such criticism from someone I would expect would be in support of my efforts to seek justice for Melissa. The emotions stirred from this incident naturally led me to a deeper contemplation about the dynamics within Melissa's circle of friends. It raised valid questions about whether there might be individuals who held information or secrets relevant to the case they have not yet shared with law enforcement.

In cases as complex as Melissa's, it's not uncommon for individuals close to the victim to hold back information, whether out of fear, loyalty, guilt, or even the belief that what they know might not be significant. Over time, relationships evolve, and the weight of holding on to potentially crucial information can become more burdensome, possibly leading some to reconsider their silence.

This email served as a reminder of the importance of re-examining the relationships and interactions surrounding Melissa at the time of her murder. So I reached out to Melissa's friends and acquaintances once again, offering a safe and confidential space for them to share any information, no matter how insignificant it may seem. I knew that even the smallest detail that was previously overlooked or deemed irrelevant in the past could be the key to unlocking new leads in the investigation.

As I engaged with Melissa's circle of friends and acquaintances, a recurring theme began to emerge that centered around the unnamed suspect's concerning pattern of harassment and aggression. One woman confided in me that he had physically damaged her property in such a brazen manner she was convinced he had no regard for the safety of others or for the law. She never reported the crime, because she feared for her life.

Story after story unfolded, each revealing more about his foul deeds. These accounts painted a picture of a person capable of causing significant harm, and they began to form a mosaic of evidence that suggested he was capable of murder. Each narrative added to the growing call for accountability, ensuring that the suspect's actions would not go unanswered.

The challenge ahead lay in meticulously piecing together these stories, corroborating details, and constructing a timeline that could place the suspect at the center of the investigation. With each new account, the path to justice for Melissa Witt became clearer, promising that the truth would eventually surface, and her memory would be honored with the resolution her case deserved.

The hurtful comment on Facebook, initially a source of distress, inadvertently became yet another catalyst for an important fact-finding mission that gave me even more information about the man I believe killed Melissa Witt. This signified a pivotal moment in my investigation, underscoring the possibility that individuals within Melissa's social circle or those acquainted with the unnamed suspect might hold critical pieces of the puzzle needed to advance the case.

The idea that "someone knows" seemed to be coming to fruition. I wondered if the unnamed suspect could feel the ground shift as his secrets were slowly being unearthed. The sprouts of justice were growing—promising to expose the truth of who killed Melissa Witt.

Someone knows what he did, I thought to myself, *and it's only a matter of time before I find them.*

Chapter 27: I Think He Did It

"Alexa, play Taylor Swift," I commanded as I chopped vegetables in my kitchen, preparing dinner for my large family. Seconds later, the lyrics to "No Body, No Crime" rang through the air, and my daughters and I immediately sang along: "I think he did it but I just can't prove it. I think he did it but I just can't prove it." As we belted out the lyrics to Swift's song, without warning, my 16-year-old, Paige, blurted out: "This reminds me of you and the Witt case, Mom. I think you know who did it—and it scares me that you might know a real life murderer, Mom!"

The room fell silent, the playful ambiance replaced by a palpable tension. I glanced over at Paige, her eyes wide with a mix of curiosity and concern. I wiped my hands on a dish towel, took a deep breath, and gently pulled her into an embrace. "You don't have to worry about that, okay?"

"I do worry about it, Mom," she confided. "This work seems dangerous."

"I didn't realize you worried about this Witt case" I said, leaning against the kitchen counter. The younger girls looked confused, but Paige nodded, so I continued. "I do think I know who murdered her, so I guess that is a little bit scary. And even though we can't prove who killed her yet, we will someday. We are very close."

Paige's interest was piqued. "So, did you think you've talked to Melissa's killer?"

I sighed as I pictured the unnamed suspect's face. "I think I have, yes."

"But how do you deal with that? Knowing he's out there, free because you can't prove anything?" Paige's voice trembled slightly, a mix of fear and awe in her tone.

I looked at her, then at all my daughters, and saw the concern in their eyes. "It's tough, but it's part of the job. We do our best with what we have and, sometimes, justice takes a little longer to serve. The important thing is to never give up, to keep searching for the truth, no matter how hard it might be."

Dinner continued with more questions about the Witt case, the challenges and the small victories. We discussed the importance of perseverance, integrity, and the relentless pursuit of truth. As we cleared the table, Paige hugged me tightly. "I'm proud of you, Mom. I hope you get justice for Melissa."

After my children went to bed that night, I thought about the Witt case and the unnamed suspect. Maybe it was time to revisit some old leads, to dig a little deeper. Inspired by the resilience I wanted to instill in my daughters, I realized that some cases, like seeds of truth, just need a little more time to break through the surface.

And with that thought, I knew I couldn't rest until the Witt case was closed, once and for all.

I pored over my notes again, and I reread the FBI's profile for the suspect: a male, likely a loner with a history of troubled relationships. He would possess a deep-seated resentment toward women, possibly stemming from past rejections. The profile suggested he most likely thrived on a sense of control, was a macho man with many girlfriends, a police-groupie, and a sportsman.

As I dug deeper into our unnamed suspect's life, he was a man who, on paper, seemed to embody the very essence of the FBI's profile. He had a history of volatile relationships, and he was notorious for stringing along multiple women at one time. He was an avid outdoorsman who admitted to spending a great deal of time in the Ozark National Forest, and, of course, he knew Melissa Witt. But it was his propensity for violence—for attempting to strangle his ex-girlfriends when he was angry, combined with Nixon O'Neil's description of the Mickey Mouse Watch on display in his apartment, that cemented my suspicions.

D's life, a patchwork of red flags, was hidden behind a facade of deceitful charm and striking good looks. His history with women, however, revealed the truth: a turbulent undercurrent of aggression and manipulation. His past, a litany of short-lived and tumultuous relationships, was marked by allegations of emotional and physical abuse. More than one ex-girlfriend had whispered rumors of his dark moods, of moments when disagreement turned to danger and love to fear.

During one of our late-night phone calls, D himself expressed his love of the great outdoors, particularly the Ozark National Forest, a sprawling wilderness where he claimed to find solace away from the chaos of everyday life. It was this detail that initially drew my attention, because I knew that Melissa Witt had frequented a town skirting the edges of that very forest.

But what transformed suspicion into near certainty was the account of Nixon O'Neil, a former roommate of the unnamed suspect, who had become increasingly disturbed by his behavior. Nixon's recounting of a Mickey Mouse watch, displayed almost like a trophy on a shelf, sent chills down my spine—Melissa Witt had been wearing a Mickey Mouse watch the day she was murdered, and law enforcement has long believed the killer kept her watch as a memento.

This information, combined with the witness who had been at the bowling alley on the night of Melissa's disappearance and vividly remembered her arguing with an aggressor—a man whose name began with the letter D—was enough to direct all eyes on our unnamed suspect.

"I think he did it but I just can't prove it"—the phrase from Swift's song seems to perfectly capture the frustration and challenge we are facing in this complex investigation. There is a strong amount of circumstantial evidence that points toward our unnamed suspect's guilt—much more than what I am allowed to pen within the pages of this book. And yet, despite our best efforts, undeniable proof remains elusive. Regardless, we will not give up.

We will continue re-examining evidence, exploring new angles, and we will keep waiting for new technology or information to come to light that can turn suspicion into certainty.

Patience and diligence has become as crucial in this case as the evidence itself. Each piece of information, no matter how small, could be the key to unraveling the truth. Our focus now is to piece together the puzzle, one fragment at a time, never losing sight of the ultimate goal: to bring closure to the case and justice for Melissa. I remain steadfast in my resolve to keep this investigation alive— and I will push through every obstacle and challenge until the truth is revealed.

Chapter 28: A Message From Boyd and Rider

When retired detectives Chris Boyd and Jay C. Rider asked to include a direct message from them to Melissa's killer in the final pages of this book, I did not hesitate to agree. Their request is a powerful declaration of their unwavering commitment to solving Melissa's murder. Their words are a testament to the dedication that drives the pursuit for justice in Melissa's case, even three decades after the crime was committed.

Their message, I believe, serves as a chilling reminder to the perpetrator that time does not erase guilt, nor does it diminish the resolve of those who care so deeply about this case. It's a stark reminder of the lengths to which dedicated individuals will go to bring closure to a case and how, even in retirement, their thirst for justice remains unquenched.

To Our Unnamed Suspect,
It does not take a genius to know that you read
every single word LaDonna pens. Her books are both

a blessing and a curse—they serve as fodder as you relieve the crime while simultaneously striking fear into your heart. As she speaks directly to you in this book, does your mind race back to December 1994? Do you worry about the evidence you left behind? You should.

We know who you are. A coward whose name starts with the letter D.

The answer to Melissa's murder is simple. There is no elaborate narrative at play here, no "intricate plot" or "twists and turns" as seen in cinematic tales. Most murders are committed by someone the victim knows. Someone like you.

As we replay the recording of one of your late night phone calls with LaDonna, a question you asked caught our attention. What was the motive for Melissa's murder? You already know the answer to that question—and so do we.

Do you feel uncomfortable yet? If not, you should. We know who you are.

We see you.

Do you dream about the day this finally ends? That day of reckoning is coming. We dream of it, too.

Have you asked yourself why two old investigators are still on your heels? The answer is simple: Melissa Witt deserves justice.

The day we read her diary, filled with the innocent musings of a 19-year-old, it transformed the investigation for us. Each entry, written with the carefree hope and boundless dreams characteristic of an innocent young woman, stood in stark contrast to the grim reality of what you did to her that cold December night. Her diary is a reminder of the life that was so cruelly snatched away, each page a testament to a future that will never be realized.

As we read through her words, we found ourselves not just investigators but guardians of her memory. Her words motivate us to redouble our efforts to piece together the fragmented evidence, so we can give a voice to the young woman who can no longer speak for herself.

You will not benefit from the passage of time and the burden of old age—neither has dampened our tenacity or enthusiasm. We cannot rest until you are behind bars. We will not rest. We're still here. And we're still coming for you.

—Jay C. Rider, Chris Boyd

Chapter 29: Connections

As I complete this third book dedicated to the Witt case, a significant milestone in my journey comes to a close. Writing these books have not only contributed to keeping Melissa's case in the public eye, but they have also served as a profound personal endeavor—intertwining my life with the quest for justice for a girl I never knew in a way that few can truly understand.

It is my hope that the discussions my books have sparked, the interest they've renewed, and the attention they've drawn to the case will continue to influence and inspire actions and revelations in ways that are yet to unfold.

I remain hopeful that advancements in forensic science, particularly DNA technology, along with the meticulous re-examination of physical evidence, and the potential for new witnesses to come forward as public interest in the case is at an all-time high—will all contribute to the possibility of a breakthrough.

Resolution in cases like that of Tonya Ethridge McKinley's after 35 years exemplifies the profound impact of forensic advancements on solving cold cases. Tonya, a young mother of only 23, met a horrific end in Pensacola, having been strangled and sexually assaulted after leaving a New Year's Eve celebration. The long years that followed without answers were agonizing for her family, filled with unresolved questions and a yearning for justice.

A breakthrough in that case came in March 2020, when DNA evidence, obtained from a discarded cigarette, pointed authorities to Daniel Leonard Wells, who was 57 at the time. This pivotal moment underscores the importance of even the smallest piece of evidence in a criminal investigation. A discarded cigarette, seemingly inconsequential at the moment it was dropped, became the key to unlocking a mystery that had remained unsolved for over three decades.

Wells' identification as the suspect in this case highlights the persistence of law enforcement and their dedication to leveraging new technologies and methods to solve crimes. The utilization of DNA evidence, particularly from sources that may not have been considered significant at the time of the crime, demonstrates the evolving nature of forensic science and its increasing ability to bring closure to cases long thought unsolvable.

And while the arrest of Wells could not bring Tonya back, it did provide a sense of justice and accountability that had been missing for so many years—a reminder of the lasting impact of violent crimes on the loved ones of the victims and the importance of relentless pursuit of justice, no matter how much time has passed.

I also find hope in the sentencing of Daniel Rees to 30 years to life for the 1991 murder of Rachael Johnson. Rees' sentencing brought a long-awaited resolution to a case that haunted the Akron, Ohio community and Johnson's family for over three decades. The guilty plea, part of an agreement that altered the underlying offense and spared Rees the possibility of a death sentence, marked the end of a painful chapter for all involved, although the scars of such a brutal crime will undoubtedly linger.

The tragic details of Rachael Johnson's death—blunt force trauma, sexual assault, multiple stab wounds, and being set on fire—paint a horrifying picture of the violence she endured. Much like the Witt case, the brutality of her murder not only devastated her family but left a lasting impact on the community.

The arrest of Rees, decades after the crime, was also attributed to the role of DNA technology. The link to Rees through the DNA of distant relatives highlights the growing importance of genetic genealogy in the field of criminal justice, offering hope to countless families seeking answers in unsolved cases. This breakthrough in the Johnson case serves as a testament to the persistence of law enforcement and the evolving tools at their disposal.

The involvement of Rees in the victim's life, however peripherally, as a friend of Rachael's daughter and a co-worker of her sister, adds a layer of betrayal to the already tragic circumstances. The fact that Rees had no significant criminal history and was not initially a suspect in the case is a stark reminder that the perpetrators of such crimes can sometimes hide in plain sight, eluding detection for years or even decades.

As I contemplate these cases in relation to Melissa Witt's murder, I am reminded of a crucial point: The path to justice, though sometimes long and fraught with challenges, is continuously evolving. Each cold case that is solved brings us closer to understanding how to effectively tackle others, including Melissa Witt's.

The growing community of investigators, advocates, family members, and concerned citizens in Melissa Witt's case are critical to achieving justice. Our relentless pursuit, supported by the collective wisdom and experience gained from other cases, forms a formidable front against the silence that shrouds Melissa's murder. My books on the Witt case have gone far beyond my wildest imagination— and have brought together a global community that has linked arms in a shared commitment that ensures the pursuit of truth never ceases.

Now, the legacy of my work, should it persist, must be carried on by the readers. It is up to you to stand up and demand justice for Melissa Witt.

As I move forward, it is my intent to find new paths to explore, new stories to tell, and new ways to contribute to other cold cases that deserve justice. The end of this book is not a conclusion, but a transition—an opportunity to embrace new challenges, knowing that the work I've done has made a meaningful difference.

Nearing the completion of this third book in this series dedicated to Melissa's memory, my nights were filled with vivid dreams, echoes of the journey I had undertaken. One night, as the gentle hum of the world faded into the quietude of slumber, I found myself in a dream unlike any other: I was a 90-year-old woman, standing at the precipice of eternity—at the gates of heaven itself. Before me lay a golden shore, stretching infinitely, its beauty beyond words, shimmering under a celestial light that seemed to dance upon the air.

As I took my first tentative steps across this hallowed ground, a figure in the distance caught my eye—a young woman, her presence radiating a warmth and energy that beckoned me closer. There was a familiarity in the way she stood, an anticipation in her posture that spoke of long-awaited reunion and conversation.

With each step, my heart grew lighter, the years and burdens I had carried seeming to fall away like leaves in autumn. The young woman's excitement mirrored the emotions swirling within me, a tumult of hope and of an indescribable sense of coming home.

As the distance between us dwindled, she ran toward me, her movements graceful and filled with an exuberance that belied the serene surroundings. Her hands reached for mine, her touch gentle yet filled with understanding, a connection forged through time, pain, and the shared pursuit of truth.

"Hi, I'm Melissa," she said, her voice imbued with the melody of a thousand unspoken words, a greeting that felt like a balm to the soul. In that moment, within the dreamscape of a world beyond, Melissa Witt stood before me, not as a memory or a case to be solved, but as a person, vibrant and alive, her spirit untethered by the tragedies of the past.

Her eyes, bright with the promise of youth and the wisdom of the ages, held mine, and in their depths, I found the closure I had sought for so long, not just for myself, but for all those who had come to know Melissa through the pages of my books, and my endless quest for justice.

This dream, as ephemeral as it was profound, marked the culmination of a journey that had spanned almost a decade of my life. It was a reassurance that Melissa's story would continue to resonate, to inspire, and to serve as a beacon of hope and resilience. As I awoke, the golden shore and the sound of Melissa's voice lingered, a gentle reminder that some connections, some stories, transcend the boundaries of time and space, forever etched in the annals of our hearts.

Epilogue: Justice for Dana Stidham

The dim light of the late afternoon sun filtered through the blinds of the Fort Smith Police Department conference room, as Amy and I poured over the expansive case file of Melissa Witt, its pages a testament to years of investigative work and a relentless pursuit for justice. The weight of the unsolved case lay heavy in the room, a tangible presence that fueled our determination.

As we methodically reviewed the documents, Amy's keen eyes caught a name that momentarily paused the rhythm of our work: Dana Stidham. The mention of another young life cut tragically short sent a chill through the air, intertwining the fate of two strangers in the labyrinth of unsolved crimes.

We took a moment to delve into the narrative surrounding Dana Stidham's murder in 1989, a case that emanated from the quiet town of Bella Vista, Arkansas. Dana, like Melissa, had a future brimming with possibilities that would never come to fruition. The parallels between the two cases were haunting—both young women, both lives brutally ended, leaving communities shattered and families grasping for answers in the wake of their loss.

We discovered that investigators had explored the possibility of a connection between Melissa Witt's and Dana Stidham's cases, a lead that hinted at a darkness lurking within the region, capable of such heinous acts.

Amy and I exchanged a look, a silent communication honed through countless hours of shared investigations. The inclusion of Dana's case in the Melissa Witt file was more than a mere footnote; it was a thread that, if pulled, might unravel a new mystery for us to tackle.

We quickly learned that the 1989 murder of Dana Stidham remained a haunting chapter in the small town of Bella Vista's history, a tragic story that lingers in the minds of residents and investigators alike. Dana, just 19 years old at the time of her disappearance, was last seen on July 25, 1989, after picking up some items from a local grocery store. Her absence quickly alarmed those who knew her, leading to an extensive search that gripped the community.

Weeks after her disappearance, the discovery of Dana's remains in a secluded area near Hiwasse, not far from Bella Vista, confirmed the worst fears of her family and the community. The condition of the remains and the evidence gathered from the scene pointed to a brutal murder.

The investigation into Dana's murder was exhaustive, with law enforcement exploring various leads, suspects, and theories. The community was shaken by the brutality of the crime and the thought that someone among them could be responsible for such an act. Over the years, the case saw periods of intense scrutiny and public interest, with various individuals coming under suspicion. Yet no definitive suspect was conclusively identified, and the case eventually grew cold.

The connection explored between Dana Stidham's murder and other cases, such as that of Melissa Witt, highlights the efforts by investigators to find patterns, links, or similarities that might lead to a breakthrough. In the realm of unsolved crimes, especially those involving young victims and violent circumstances, law enforcement agencies often look for potential overlaps in modus operandi, geographic proximity, and victim profile in the hope of uncovering new leads or identifying a serial offender.

Despite the initial speculation and the similarities that prompted a closer look—such as the victims' ages, the brutal nature of their murders, and the geographical proximity of where the crimes occurred—Jay C. Rider and his team ultimately found no concrete link between the two deaths.

The mention of the Stidham murder also triggered a significant memory from the early days of my involvement in the Witt case. This recollection was of a clandestine meeting that had taken place years ago, one that had almost faded into the backdrop of countless interviews, tips, and leads I had pursued over the years.

The man who had reached out to me was someone deeply engrossed in the investigation of Dana Stidham's murder. His approach was intense, his dedication evident in the way he spoke and the depth of his inquiries. He had chosen the food court at the NWA mall for our meeting—a bustling, anonymous space where conversations could blend into the background noise, away from prying eyes and ears.

During our meeting, he handed over a file that was thick with the weight of his exhaustive research. It contained hundreds of pages of meticulously gathered information, notes, and theories regarding Dana's murder. The pages were a testament to his commitment to uncovering the truth, each one filled with a mix of official documents, personal observations, and potential leads that he had painstakingly compiled.

After concluding our intensive work on the Witt case that afternoon, Amy and I felt a sense of urgency to look into Dana Stidham's case further. As we journeyed back to Northwest Arkansas, the memory of the covert meeting and the mysterious file that was handed to me years ago had resurfaced with new significance, compelling us to revisit the information with fresh eyes and renewed perspective.

Upon our return, we headed straight to my office, a space cluttered with the remnants of countless investigations, each file and note a story of its own. The atmosphere was thick with anticipation as we navigated through the maze of paperwork and personal mementos that marked my years of dedication to uncovering truths hidden in the shadows.

The back of the filing cabinet, a dusty repository of long-forgotten documents and cases, held the elusive file—a tangible link to a past effort to untangle the web of mystery surrounding Dana Stidham's murder. As I retrieved the file, its weight felt heavy with the potential to shed light on dark corners yet unexplored.

The file was as I remembered it, its pages packed with an array of information ranging from official investigation reports to handwritten notes, newspaper clippings, and maps marked with annotations. Each piece of paper was a fragment of a larger puzzle, a testament to a relentless search for justice for Dana Stidham.

Amy and I carefully spread the documents across my desk, our minds racing with the possibilities that lay before us. The information, once a secondary consideration overshadowed by the pressing demands of the Witt case, now demanded our full attention. We knew that within these pages might lie overlooked clues, patterns, or connections that could breathe new life into the Stidham case, or perhaps even intersect with other unsolved mysteries we had encountered.

As we delved into the file, the sense of connection between past and present, between the efforts of one dedicated individual and our own pursuit of justice, was overwhelming. The mysterious file, once hidden in the shadows of a filing cabinet, now lay open before us, its secrets ready to be unraveled. And so, with deep breaths and steadfast resolve, we began to sift through the pages.

Suddenly, Amy lifted her gaze to meet mine. Her eyes, usually a wellspring of determination, now reflected a depth of resolve that resonated with the gravity of our newfound mission. "Justice for Dana Stidham," she said, her voice steady—a declaration, a vow that seemed to fill the room, imbuing the space with a sense of solemnity and purpose.

And just like that, the path before us shifted. The weight of the file in our hands, once a relic of a seemingly unrelated investigation, had seamlessly woven itself into the fabric of our journey. Dana's story, her untimely and tragic end, demanded our attention, beckoning us to lend our voices to her silent plea for justice.

The decision was unspoken, yet clear between us. We had embarked on countless investigations, each with its own set of challenges and heartaches, but the call to action for Dana Stidham's case struck a chord that resonated with our deepest convictions. The pursuit of justice for one was inextricably linked to the pursuit of justice for all, and Dana's unresolved murder was a clarion call we could not ignore.

With renewed vigor and a shared sense of commitment, we began to organize the information, to chart a course through the labyrinth of leads, testimonies, and evidence that the file presented. Our work on the Witt case had honed our skills, sharpened our intuition, and strengthened our partnership, preparing us for the journey ahead.

The quest for justice for Dana Stidham was not just our mission; it was a solemn pledge to seek answers, to illuminate the truth, and to ensure that Dana's voice, though silenced, would be heard once more.

Afterword

Stepping into the public eye, especially in the pursuit of justice for those silenced by crime, is akin to navigating the unpredictable waters of a vast and often tumultuous sea. The journey, while noble, is seldom smooth, marked by the rise and fall of public opinion and the occasional tempest of dissent. It is within this complex landscape that, as I write this chapter, I have found myself.

Encountering opposition has always accompanied me like a silent shadow along my journey. However, the recent rise of factions driven by hostility has introduced a new level of challenge. These are not merely individuals with contrasting opinions, but cohesive groups bound by disdain, often vocal and unyielding in their attempts to thwart my endeavors. Their onslaught has been relentless, prompting me to confront this head-on within the concluding pages of my book as my only viable recourse. Early on in my work on the Witt case, the Fort Smith Police Department, recognizing my expertise and the critical need for modern technological intervention, entrusted me with invaluable video evidence. This footage, a silent witness to the unresolved narratives of the case, was archaic in its current form, its secrets veiled by the limitations of outdated technology. Understanding its potential to cast light on the darkest corners of the investigation, I offered to take on the significant task of updating the crime scene footage to newer technology. This was not just a technical upgrade but a move meant to ensure the evidence could speak its truth more clearly.

However, within the intricate web of professional alliances and rivalries, not all eyes viewed this entrusted role with respect and understanding. Among my team, one figure stood out, not for her contributions to the case but for the shadows of envy and discontent that seemed to follow her. This woman, seemingly driven by a complex web of personal grievances and professional jealousy, has viewed my role through a distorted lens of suspicion and resentment.

One chilling morning, as the team gathered to discuss the progress of their efforts our progress, we discovered that she had unleashed the tempest of her rage within the walls of the Fort Smith Police Department. With accusations as sharp as ice, she alleged that I had stolen the video evidence. The words, fueled by an unfounded jealous rage, hung heavy in the air as she tried to cast a pall of doubt and uncertainty over my integrity and the team's morale.

Yet, the truth, steadfast and unmarred by the tumult of human emotions, lay in the clear facts of the situation. I am far from the thief she painted me to be. The truth is that our efforts to update the video footage to newer technology was the linchpin in a critical endeavor sanctioned by the highest echelons of the Fort Smith Police Department. The project to modernize the crime scene footage was not only approved by law enforcement, but was also supported financially by my team, underlining our commitment to shedding light on the truth.

Upon the completion of this critical task, I then took the next decisive step. Understanding the importance of transparency and collaboration in such intricate investigations, I arranged for both the original and the updated footage to be handed over to the lead on Melissa's unsolved case at the time–Detective Troy Williams.

My commitment to facilitating a smooth investigative process did not stop at merely handing over the footage. In an era where technology could bridge gaps and expedite justice, I also proposed an innovative plan to ensure that the footage was not only accessible but also easily reviewable by the key stakeholders. A private YouTube channel became the chosen medium——a secure digital space where barriers to access were meticulously dismantled, ensuring that the footage was readily available to both my team and the law enforcement officers dedicated to the case.

This digital repository was no ordinary YouTube channel. It was a fortress of confidentiality, its gates opened only to those who were directly involved in peeling back the layers of the Witt case. The creation of the private YouTube channel has been a breakthrough, a critical move orchestrated to ensure that the updated footage was accessible only to those directly involved in the Witt case. The agreement was clear and binding: the content, both the videos and any still images derived from them, was restricted exclusively to my documentary team and law enforcement personnel. This safeguard was put in place not just as a measure of security, but as a testament to the trust and responsibility bestowed upon my team by the Fort Smith Police Department. The decision to use such a platform was strategic, enabling Detective Williams and his team to view the footage at their convenience, to pause, rewind, and dissect every frame with the precision that the case demanded.

As the footage went live on this secure channel, it marked a significant milestone in the investigation. The grainy, flickering images of the past were transformed into clear, accessible evidence, their silent narratives now whispering truths that had the potential to steer the direction of the case.

Yet, within every story of progress and dedication, there often lies a twist of fate—a moment that tests the very foundations of trust and integrity. And for me and my team, this moment came with a startling betrayal. This woman, whose envy had previously clouded her judgment, found herself at a crossroads. Her continuous outlandish assumptions about the case, coupled with her inability to collaborate constructively, led to her inevitable dismissal from my team. This decision, though difficult, was necessary to maintain the integrity and focus of the investigation for our documentary.

Fueled by resentment and a desire to retaliate, this woman chose a path of deception. In a dramatic turn, she approached law enforcement, spinning a tale far removed from reality. She claimed that the sacred agreement had been breached, that the evidence had not only been stolen but had been shown to dozens of people outside the agreed-upon circle.

This accusation sent shockwaves through the team and law enforcement. The trust that had been carefully built, the progress that had been made, was suddenly under threat. Faced with these serious allegations, the Fort Smith Police Department was compelled to scrutinize the situation closely.

The storm of accusations reached a crescendo, compelling law enforcement to call for a meeting that would bring me face-to-face with detectives in Fort Smith. The gravity of this the situation was not lost on me; the very foundation of my work and my team's integrity were at stake. Yet, amidst the swirling doubts and the weight of accusations, my resolve was unshaken.

During the meeting, the first thing I did was address the elephant in the room—the conflict with this woman that had escalated beyond professional disagreements and had culminated in her dismissal from the team. I provided a detailed account, supported by documentation, of the events leading up to our falling out. This narrative was crucial, not only in shedding light on the motivations behind her allegations but also in framing the context in which they were made. The documents painted a picture of a disagreement rooted in unprofessional conduct and a risk to the integrity of the project, leading to an unavoidable but justified separation.

The crux of my defense, however, lay in the evidence surrounding the handling and dissemination of the updated footage. With meticulous detail, I presented logs and records that unequivocally showed the footage's viewership was strictly limited to the intended audience— my team and Detective Williams' and his colleagues. This was a vital piece of evidence, directly countering the accusations of widespread unauthorized sharing.

The YouTube channel, a pivotal element in this narrative, was scrutinized in detail. I revealed that the video, the subject of much controversy, had been viewed a mere five times before it was removed. This fact was not just a number; it was a testament to the controlled and responsible management of sensitive evidence. The limited viewership corroborated my assertions that the footage was shared with a select few, underpinning the integrity of my team's actions.

Investigators listened intently, the weight of each piece of evidence not lost on them. The documentation of my team's internal conflict, the meticulous viewership logs, and the restrained use of the YouTube channel spoke volumes. They collectively painted a picture of a team that, despite internal challenges, remained steadfast in its commitment to maintaining the integrity and confidentiality of crucial evidence.

The revelations brought forth in the meeting began to dissipate the cloud of suspicion that had loomed over me and my team. The evidence was clear, tangible, and a vindication not just of my character but of the entire team's dedication to our cause and the ethical standards we have worked hard to uphold.

As the meeting drew to a close, the air of tension that had once filled the room gave way to a sense of resolution. Investigators, now equipped with a comprehensive understanding of the situation, acknowledged the baselessness of the accusations. The clarity brought forth by my presentation reaffirmed the trust between law enforcement and my team, a crucial element in our continued collaboration on the Witt case.

I emerged from that meeting with the weight of the unfounded accusations lifted from my shoulders. The presentation of evidence and the transparent account of my team's actions had paved the way for understanding and vindication. The sense of relief that washed over me was palpable, a momentary balm to the wounds inflicted by weeks of suspicion and doubt.

In the immediate aftermath, there was a sense of closure, a belief that the storm had passed and that the truth had unequivocally prevailed. The integrity of my work and my team's commitment had been recognized and reaffirmed by law enforcement, a validation that felt like a beacon of hope in the murky waters of the Witt case.

However, the tranquility and sense of resolution that followed the meeting were not to last. This woman, undeterred by the outcomes of the official inquiry and seemingly fueled by a vendetta that went beyond professional disagreements, refused to let the matter rest. Her departure from the team had left a scar, one that she wore as a badge of defiance, channeling her bitterness into a campaign of sustained malice.

The realization that the vindication within the walls of the law enforcement meeting was not a panacea was sobering. The battle for truth was not confined to presenting evidence and countering accusations in official inquiries. It extended into the community, into the hearts and minds of those who had, over time, become part of the narrative of the Witt case.

Following my unwavering defense and the law enforcement meeting that vindicated my team from any wrongdoing, a fresh wave of challenges emerged. Frustrated by her inability to smear my reputation and undermine the diligent efforts of my team, this woman has resorted to new tactics to fuel her vendetta. That is why it is imperative for me to reassure my loyal readers that this issue has once again been brought to the attention of the Fort Smith Police Department. I recently escalated the matter to Captain Wendell Sampson, the same officer who initially addressed this situation when it first arose.

You can be confident that my relationship with the Fort Smith Police Department remains strong, and I am actively pursuing measures to definitively resolve this issue.

Now that this matter has been addressed, I urge you to shift your focus to the essential issue: securing justice for Melissa Ann Witt. The *unidentified suspect* discussed in these pages may become more prone to errors now that suspicion hangs over him. Stay vigilant for any such missteps and persevere in our joint pursuit of justice. If you possess any information, please step forward and reach out to Detective Brad Marion at the Fort Smith Police Department. Melissa Witt deserves nothing less than full justice, and, together, let's ensure she receives it.

Acknowledgements

To my husband, Danny: From the outset, when the Witt case was just a whisper of injustice that stirred something deep within me, you were there. Your unwavering belief in the pursuit of truth became the bedrock on which I built my resolve. It was your gentle encouragement on the daunting days that reminded me why this journey mattered, not just to me, but to all those touched by Melissa's story.

You have been my confidant, my sounding board, and my sanctuary. When the threads of the investigation tangled, you were there to help unravel them, offering insights that only someone who knew me so intimately could provide. Your keen intellect and compassionate heart often guided me back to the path when the way seemed lost.

Writing the books was a venture we embarked on *together*, even though your name does not grace the covers. Long nights spent at the keyboard were made bearable by your presence, a comforting steadiness in the tumultuous sea of emotions that the case has evoked. You were the first to read each chapter, providing feedback that was both critical and kind, pushing me to delve deeper and to write not just with my mind but with my heart.

Your sacrifices have not gone unnoticed. The countless hours you spent taking care of the kids by yourself while I was engrossed in my work have made this possible—thank you. You have been a silent pillar of strength that has allowed me to chase the whispers of justice in a noisy world.

But perhaps the most profound support you have offered has been in your ability to remind me of life beyond this case. In moments of despair or obsession, you gently pulled me back to reality. You have taught me that the pursuit of justice, while noble, should not consume the beauty of the present, that our quest was not just about honoring the past but about cherishing our time together in the present.

As I pen my gratitude, I realize that words can scarcely capture the depth of my appreciation. Your role in this journey was not just supportive; it was transformative. It was your love, patience, and unwavering support that made it possible for me to pursue justice for Melissa Witt and share her story with the world.

I owe a debt of gratitude that I can only hope to repay by honoring the love and support you've given me so freely. Together, we have traversed the darkest of waters, and in doing so, we have kept the light of hope and justice burning bright. Thank you, from the bottom of my heart, for being the unsung hero in this story, and for every moment, every sacrifice, and every word of encouragement that made this journey possible.

To Jay C. Rider and Chris Boyd: As I pause to reflect on the monumental contributions of these two remarkable men to the Witt case, I have to mention that their tireless dedication and unwavering commitment to justice have not only propelled this investigation forward but have also deeply inspired the narrative that unfolds within these pages.

Jay C. Rider, with his seasoned insight and steadfast resolve, has been a beacon of hope in the often murky waters of this case. His intuitive approach to the intricacies of investigative work, coupled with a profound empathy for the victims and their families, has illuminated paths that were once shrouded in shadow. His ability to weave together disparate threads of evidence, to see beyond the surface and into the heart of the matter, has been instrumental in my understanding of the case's complexities.

Chris Boyd, with his meticulous attention to detail and a relentless pursuit of truth, has been another pillar in this arduous journey. His expertise and dedication have brought clarity to the chaos, offering new perspectives and uncovering hidden facets of the investigation that have been crucial to our progress. Chris's commitment to the cause, his refusal to let the passage of time diminish the urgency of justice, has been a powerful motivator, reminding me of the importance of perseverance.

Together, Jay C. and Chris have embodied the essence of what it means to be guardians of justice. Their partnership, marked by mutual respect and a shared vision, has not only advanced the investigation but has also served as a profound example of collaboration in the face of adversity.

As I weave their contributions and experiences into the fabric of this book, I am filled with a deep sense of gratitude. Their stories, fraught with challenges and marked by moments of breakthrough, have provided a rich tapestry of insight and inspiration. It is through their eyes that we gain a deeper understanding of the complexities of this case, and it is through their efforts that we are reminded of the enduring impact of dedicated public service.

This book serves as a tribute to your unwavering commitment and tireless efforts in the pursuit of justice for Melissa Witt and countless others whose voices you have fought to amplify. Your legacy is not only etched in the annals of law enforcement but is also deeply honored in these pages.

Thank you, Jay C. and Chris, for your invaluable contributions, your friendship, your unrelenting spirit, and the profound difference you have made not only in my life but in the lives of so many touched by tragedy. Your dedication has not only propelled this investigation forward but has also inspired a narrative of hope, resilience, and the relentless pursuit of truth.

I will carry the lessons you have taught me about investigative work and friendship for the rest of my life. It is an honor to call you both my mentors and two of my best friends.

To Lexi Kakis: In the journey of bringing this book to life, a journey marked by moments of profound discovery and poignant reflection on the Melissa Witt case, one beacon of light has stood unwaveringly by my side: Lexi Kakis. This tribute is a testament to her invaluable love, support, and the critical role she has played in the creation of this narrative.

Lexi, with her boundless compassion and insightful perspectives, has been more than just a supporter; she has been a cornerstone of this book. From the earliest drafts to the final pages, her keen eye and empathetic heart have helped to shape the narrative, ensuring that the story told was not only true to the facts but also to the emotional landscape that defines such a profound investigation.

Her ability to listen, to truly hear the stories that lie between the lines, has been a source of comfort and inspiration. In moments of doubt or when the weight of the story seemed too heavy to bear, Lexi's encouragement was a guiding light, her belief in the importance of this work a reminder of its necessity.

Lexi's friendship, a constant presence, has provided a sanctuary for me amidst the tumult of research, interviews, and writing. Her unwavering support, her readiness to offer a word of encouragement or a moment of levity, helped to balance the scales, to bring a sense of peace to the process.

Her engagement with the book, her willingness to delve into the complexities of the case, and her thoughtful feedback were instrumental in honing the narrative. Lexi's insights, often illuminating overlooked aspects or encouraging deeper exploration, enriched the story in ways that were both subtle and significant.

But perhaps the most profound contribution Lexi has made to this journey is her understanding of the emotional toll such a narrative can exact. Her compassion, her ability to provide solace and strength, has been a wellspring of resilience, enabling me to approach the story with a sense of purpose and clarity.

Lexi, this tribute barely scratches the surface of my gratitude. Your love, support, and insightful readings of this book as it took shape have been gifts of immeasurable value. You have been an integral part of this journey, a partner in the truest sense, and for that, I am eternally grateful.

Your spirit, infused within the pages of this book, serves as a reminder of the power of empathy, the importance of support, and the incredible impact that one person's love and encouragement can have on the creation of something meant to serve a greater purpose. Thank you, Lexi, for everything.

To Amy Smith: As I sit down to reflect on the arduous journey that led to the creation of this book, and the exhaustive investigation into the Witt case that preceded it, my thoughts inevitably turn to you, my steadfast companion through it all. This tribute is but a small token of my immense gratitude for your unwavering support, invaluable assistance, and the deep friendship that has been both my anchor and my compass.

From the outset, your belief in the importance of shedding light on Melissa Witt's story mirrored my own, yet it was your unique perspective and relentless dedication that often illuminated the path forward when shadows seemed to obscure the way. Your keen insights and untiring resolve have been instrumental in piecing together fragments of a puzzle that seemed insurmountable at times.

Your role in this journey has been multifaceted; you were at once a confidante, a sounding board, and a co-investigator. The countless hours we spent sifting through evidence, debating theories, and tracing leads were made not only bearable but meaningful because of your presence. Your ability to listen, to truly understand the nuances of the case, and to offer thoughtful, critical feedback was a beacon of hope in moments of doubt.

But beyond the investigative work, it was your emotional support that became my stronghold. The weight of the stories we delved into, the tragedy and injustice we encountered, often threatened to become overwhelming. Yet, in those moments, your friendship offered a sanctuary, a place of solace and strength where I could find respite.

As I wrote this book, your encouragement was a constant source of inspiration. Your unwavering belief in the significance of this work, and in my ability to bring it to fruition, was a gift of immeasurable value.

Your contribution to this journey extends far beyond the tangible assistance you provided. This book that stands as a testament to our shared commitment to justice and truth is also a tribute to the enduring power of friendship.

Words cannot fully capture the depth of my gratitude, nor the profound respect I have for your intellect, your compassion, and your unwavering loyalty. This book, and the journey that led to its creation, has been immeasurably enriched by your involvement.

Thank you, from the bottom of my heart, for standing by me, for lending your strength, your wisdom, and your heart to this endeavor. Our friendship, tested and tempered by this experience, stands as a beacon of hope and a reminder of what can be achieved when we join hands in pursuit of a cause greater than ourselves.

To Steven and Leya, my esteemed publishers: In the tapestry of this journey, from the inception of an idea to the tangible reality of a published book, your role has been nothing short of transformative. This tribute is a humble attempt to convey my deepest gratitude for the faith you placed in me as a writer, for the unwavering support you've extended, and for the friendship that has blossomed amidst the professional ties that bind us.

Taking a chance on an author is no small leap of faith. It requires vision, belief in the potential of a story, and a willingness to embark on a journey. Your decision to embrace my work, to see the value in the narrative I sought to weave, has been the cornerstone of this endeavor. It was your initial trust in me that set the wheels in motion, transforming a manuscript laden with hopes and dreams into a vessel that carries a powerful story to readers far and wide.

Throughout the publishing process, your guidance has been invaluable. In the labyrinth of edits, design choices, and marketing strategies, your expertise has been a guiding light, ensuring that the book not only reached completion but soared beyond my highest expectations. Your commitment to excellence, your attention to detail, and your dedication to the craft of bringing stories to life have been instrumental in shaping the final product.

Beyond the professional support, what I cherish most is the friendship that has emerged from our collaboration. In the highs and lows that accompany the journey of bringing a book to life, your camaraderie, your shared excitement for the project, and your genuine investment in its success have been sources of immense comfort and motivation. The bond that we have formed transcends the typical author-publisher relationship, adding a layer of richness and depth to this adventure.

Your belief in my work has not only empowered me as a writer but has also instilled a sense of responsibility and drive to exceed even my own expectations. The faith you've shown in my ability to tell a story that matters, to engage with readers on topics of significance, has been a powerful catalyst for growth, both personal and professional.

As this book takes its place in the world, I am acutely aware that its journey from concept to reality is a testament to your support, your expertise, and your belief in the power of storytelling. The impact of your work extends far beyond the pages of this book; it touches the lives of every reader who finds solace, inspiration, or understanding within its chapters.

Thank you for taking a chance on me, for your ongoing support, and for the friendship that has enriched this journey beyond measure. Your role in this story is indelible, and my gratitude is boundless. Together, we have brought forth a narrative that, I hope, will resonate with readers and contribute meaningfully to the tapestry of human experience.

To my beloved children: As I pen this acknowledgment, my heart swells with a profound sense of gratitude and love for each of you. This book, a labor of love and dedication, has been shaped not just by my experiences and insights but significantly by the influence you've had on my life.

Your boundless curiosity, your laughter, and your moments of wisdom beyond your years have been a constant source of inspiration. Each question you've posed, each story you've shared, and each challenge we've navigated together has contributed to the depth and authenticity of this narrative. Your perspectives have reminded me to view the world through a lens of wonder and empathy.

The journey of writing this book has been intertwined with the journey of raising you, and it is impossible to separate the two. The late nights, the early mornings, the moments of doubt and triumph—all were witnessed by your encouraging smiles and steadfast belief in the importance of this work. Your patience and understanding, especially in times when my focus seemed divided, have been gifts of immeasurable value.

Your resilience and joy, even in the face of life's inevitable challenges, have taught me about the strength of the human spirit, a theme that resonates throughout the pages of this book. You've shown me that every story is made up of individual moments, and it is the love and courage we bring to these moments that define us.

This book is a tribute to the incredible individuals you are becoming, and to the indelible mark you've left on my heart and my work. The laughter, the tears, and the countless memories we've created together are woven into every word of this book.

Thank you for being my greatest teachers, my fiercest supporters, and the most wonderful sources of inspiration a parent could ask for. This book, and the journey it represents, is dedicated to you, with all my love and gratitude.

To Todd Matthews: This book is lovingly dedicated to the memory of Todd Matthews, a fellow advocate whose passion, dedication, and pioneering spirit in the realm of justice nearly matched my own. Todd's tireless work in bringing attention to the forgotten, giving voice to the voiceless, and his commitment to solving cold cases transformed not only the lives of the individuals and families he helped but also the very fabric of how such cases are approached and solved. His legacy is one of hope, resilience, and the profound belief that every person matters, and every story deserves a resolution.

In his honor, this book aspires to carry forward the torch of advocacy, to illuminate the dark corners of unresolved cases, and to remind us all of the power of community, compassion, and persistence in the pursuit of truth and justice.

Todd's passing is a profound loss, but his spirit and the impact of his work continue to inspire and guide us. This dedication serves as a small token of gratitude for his contributions and a commitment to continue the important work he championed with such fervor.

Todd, you were a true beacon of hope and justice—your legacy lives on in the pages of this book and in the hearts of your fellow advocates.

Jera Houghtaling, Dana Poll, Misty Sutley, Nic Edwards, Cherry, Lance Reenstierna, Rob Bacile, Healey Tonsing, Thomas Landstrum, Beth McClam, Joshua Kessler, James Renner, Tyler Allen, Brad Marion, Jo Ellison, Chad Mira, Nathan Oliver, Paul and Brenda Base, Catherine Townsend, Marlena Rider, Gavin Fish, Connor Holmes and the staff of CrimeCon U.S. and UK—*every single one of you* have played a role in supporting me on this journey for justice and I am incredibly thankful. Thank you for believing in me and standing alongside me with passion and resolve for Melissa's unsolved case. Justice is coming!

To David McClam: I cherish your love, support and friendship beyond measure. I look forward to all of the amazing things we are going to tackle together! Thank you for your presence in my life. I could not do this without you.

Last but not least, this book is dedicated to **Melissa Witt**, whose life was tragically cut short but whose spirit continues to inspire a relentless pursuit of justice. Melissa's story, marked by unspeakable tragedy, has galvanized a community of advocates, investigators, and kind-hearted souls, all united in the quest to uncover the truth and ensure that justice is served.

In her memory, this narrative seeks not only to shed light on the circumstances of her story but also to honor the vibrancy of her life, the impact she had on those who knew her, and the mark she has left on our hearts—especially mine. Melissa's legacy is a reminder of the preciousness of life, the importance of compassion, and the enduring strength of a community bound together in the face of adversity.

May this book serve as a tribute to Melissa's enduring spirit, a beacon of hope for those who seek justice, and a testament to the unyielding resolve of those who refuse to let her memory fade. In dedicating this work to Melissa, I reaffirm my commitment to seeking answers, to advocating for the voiceless, and to standing steadfast in the face of the unknown.

Melissa, though you were taken from this world too soon, your story continues to inspire change, to evoke empathy, and to rally a collective spirit of resilience. Your memory is cherished, your life celebrated, and your legacy honored through these pages and the ongoing efforts to bring peace to your story. We're going to get him, I promise.

To the man responsible for Melissa's murder, know that this story is not about granting you notoriety or a place of remembrance. Instead, it serves as a resounding declaration that the quest for justice never wanes, that the memory of the victim endures with dignity and love, and that the collective will of a community seeking answers and resolution is unbreakable.

May this book reinforce the commitment to uncovering the truth, to honoring Melissa's memory in a manner befitting her spirit, and to the belief that justice, though sometimes delayed, is an inextinguishable light in the darkness.

To Melissa's killer: your actions have left a void that can never be filled, but they have also ignited a relentless pursuit for justice. In echoing the sentiments of Jay C. Rider and Chris Boyd, I want you to know that we are not just issuing a warning; we are affirming an inevitable reality. The combined efforts of advancements in forensic science, the tireless dedication of investigators, and the unwavering support of the community are steadily closing in on you. You may have believed that you had slipped through the cracks, evading the consequences of your actions, but fate had other plans. In an unexpected twist, a mother of seven, fueled by the sheer determination to seek justice, made a solemn vow to find you. As you read the words meticulously penned within the pages of this book, the weight of realization settles upon you – I have, indeed, found you. Your days of anonymity and impunity are now numbered. Prepare yourself, for the reckoning is at hand. No corner of darkness will shield you from the light of justice.